I0015189

Machine Learning

A Technical Approach To Machine Learning For Beginners

Leonard Eddison

2

The trademarks that are used are without any consent, and the publication of the trademark is without permission or backing by the trademark owner. All trademarks and brands within this book are for clarifying purposes only and are the owned by the owners themselves, not affiliated with this document.

TABLE OF CONTENTS

Page intentionally left blank

WHAT IS MACHINE LEARNING

Machine learning is a data analytics technique that teaches computers to do what comes naturally to humans and animals: learn from experience. Machine learning algorithms use computational methods to "learn" information directly from data without relying on a predetermined equation as a model. The algorithms adaptively improve their performance as the number of samples available for learning increases.

Why does machine learning matter?

Machine learning plays a critical role in digital transformation. Across industries, organizations seek to leverage the digital revolution for more revenue or lower costs. Machine learning makes it possible for teams to work smarter, do things faster, and make previously impossible tasks routine.

How do organizations use machine learning?

Machine learning can:

• Predict a future value

• Estimate a probability

• Infer an unknown

• Classify an object

• Group similar objects together

• Detect associations

• Identify outliers

Organizations put these capabilities to work in numerous ways. For example, a retailer can use machine learning to predict the volume of traffic in a store on a given day and use that prediction to optimize staffing. A bank can use machine learning to infer the current market value of a home (based on its size, characteristics, and neighborhood); in turn, this lowers the cost of appraisals and expedites mortgage processing.

Is machine learning new?

No. Some machine learning techniques date back to the 1940s. As in any field, researchers continuously innovate. However, widely used methods such as logistic regression and decision trees are more than 50 years old.

If machine learning isn't new, why is there so much interest today?

Machine learning algorithms need a lot of data and computing power to produce useful results. Today, we have more data than ever, and computing power is pervasive and cheap. Machine learning algorithms are better than ever and widely available in open source softwares. Some well-publicized recent successes for machine learning add to the "buzz."

How does machine learning make impossible tasks routine?

Machine learning produces knowledge which organizations build into applications that can process millions of transactions at a fraction of the cost of manual handling. This capability makes it possible for businesses to do things that would be prohibitively expensive if performed by humans.

For example, consider an application that handles incoming email traffic to a customer service center. With text mining, a branch of machine learning, the app automatically responds to some emails and routes others to specialists for a response. It would be extraordinarily expensive for an organization to hire human analysts to read every incoming email. Machine learning makes possible for the center to offer a communications channel to customers at an acceptable cost.

How does machine learning work?

There are many different types of machine learning algorithms, and each class works differently. In general, machine learning algorithms begin with an initial hypothetical model, they determine how well this model fits a set of data, and improve the model iteratively. This training process continues until the algorithm can find no additional improvements, or the user stops the process.

What is the difference between statistics and machine learning?

Researchers use statistical techniques to test the hypothesis that data conforms to a known mathematical distribution, such as a linear model. Machine learning algorithms, on the other hand, seek to learn patterns that do not necessarily conform to known mathematical distributions.

Statisticians developed tools, such as linear regression, many years ago, when researchers worked with small data sets and performed computations by hand.

Today, practitioners have data and computing power that was not available to classical statisticians. While academics once debated the validity of machine learning and statistical techniques, today most data scientists freely use methods from both disciplines.

What is the difference between machine learning and artificial intelligence (AI)?

Machine learning is part of the artificial intelligence ecosystem, but AI includes additional capabilities, such as sensors, devices that interact with the natural world, and computer-based reasoning.

Autonomous vehicles offer an excellent example of applied AI. There are machine learning components built into an autonomous vehicle. But the vehicle also includes sensors that capture and encode data about the world — a "brain" that reasons and makes decisions — and devices that instruct the wheels to turn, the engine to accelerate, and so forth.

What is the difference between machine learning and deep learning?

Deep learning is a subcategory of machine learning. Neural networks are a kind of machine learning that represent knowledge as a set of mathematical functions organized in a directed graph and arranged in layers. Neural networks with multiple "hidden" layers are so-called "deep" neural networks. Deep learning is useful because it performs well on tasks such as image and speech recognition, where other machine learning techniques perform poorly.

What is the difference between machine learning and data science?

Machine learning is a technology; data science is a discipline. Data scientists use machine learning to build predictive applications.

Who creates machine learning algorithms?

Researchers and practitioners in business, government, and academia create or enhance machine learning algorithms. They publish papers that describe the benefits of each innovation.

A machine learning algorithm is only useful when it is implemented in software. Most algorithm developers choose freely available open source software for their algorithms; this facilitates broader adoption by the community.

What languages do data scientists use for machine learning?

There are machine learning libraries available for many different computer languages, including C and Java. However, the most popular languages among data scientists are Python, R, and Scala.

Does Cloudera offer tools for machine learning?

Yes. Cloudera Enterprise Data Hub includes Apache Spark, a distributed in-memory engine for high-performance data processing. Spark includes a machine learning library called MLlib, which is widely used to discover new machine learning techniques.

1. Assessing and Addressing Students' Skills and Weaknesses

Thinkster Math uses artificial intelligence and machine learning to track the steps students take while solving math problems. Students solve problems on the app, and the app produces detailed progress reports specifying their understanding of the different skills tested.. Thinkster Math matches students with online math tutors who personalize their learning programs based on the students' strengths and weaknesses, but it is also used in the classroom.

Educators use Thinkster Math to determine how students learn and comprehend math concepts so they don't fall behind. The app enables them to quickly diagnose each student's weaknesses without having to review a large stack of tests and assignments, leaving them more time to create individualized assignments that target specific skill sets.

2. Empowering Students with Crowdsourced Learning

Brainly isn't used in the classroom. Rather, the online messaging board facilitates peer-to-peer learning by making it easy for students to ask questions, connect with "friends," and have their questions answered by other students.

Brainly moderators verify questions and answers on the platform to make sure they're high-quality. The company also developed machine learning algorithms that automatically filter out spam and low-quality content, such as incorrect answers, so that moderators have more time to focus on helping students navigate the site, the Next Web reports.

Additionally, Brainly partnered with Professor Chirag Shah and Rutgers University to use machine learning to match students based on their skill sets. A student who has successfully answered advanced American history questions, for example, could be matched with a student who has questions about

American history coursework. "We start off by determining a new user's learning level by offering them easier questions to answer. Then we connect them with other, more established Brainly users who can mentor them, and then we gradually move them forward ... We're looking to spark interest and endow confidence for students who may lack interest or support," Professor Shah said on Brainly's blog.

3. Creating Customized Learning Materials

Content Technologies Inc. (CTI), an artificial intelligence research and development company, develops AI that creates customized educational content. Using deep learning to absorb and analyze existing course materials, textbooks, and syllabi, the technology creates custom learning materials, including textbooks, chapter summaries, and multiple choice tests, PCMag reports.

CTI has two additional tools: Cram101 and JustTheFacts101. Cram101 uses AI to break down existing textbooks into nuggets of information and generates study guides with chapter summaries, practice tests, and even flashcards. Similarly, JustTheFacts101 highlights pertinent information from the textbook and builds chapter summaries. These tools save time on some of the more menial study tasks — like making a mountainous stack of flashcards — so students have more time to focus on comprehending concepts.

4. Decreasing Time Spent Grading

Gradescope makes grading tests and assignments a lot faster for secondary school and higher education instructors. Students upload assignments to the Gradescope platform, and its AI capability sorts and groups answers to check multiple assignments at once. According to Gradescope, its use of AI decreases time spent grading by 70 percent or more.

Additionally, the software provides instructors with a detailed analysis on what their students got right and wrong so they can provide individualized tutoring to each student or re-teach entire concepts.

In conversations about artificial intelligence, concerns often arise about its impact on human employees. One commonality between each of these educational tools, however, is that they are used to provide value to teachers and tutors, rather than taking their place. "The way I think about it, there are seven billion people on this earth, and about half of them don't have access to good education," Professor Goel said in a conversation with Quartz. "If we can take artificial intelligence and provide those people with minimal question answering, who knows what a difference it could make in someone's life?"

2018 OUTLOOK FOR MACHINE LEARNING – AN INNOVATION IN ITS TEEN YEARS

A year ago, Gartner, the world's leading research and advisory company, named artificial intelligence (AI), machine learning (ML), and conversational systems three of the top strategic tech trends for 2017. In May last year, SAP launched the SAP Leonardo Machine Learning portfolio at SAPPHIRE NOW in Orlando, Florida, and thus demonstrated that it's on the pulse of innovation. Today, it is about time to sum up the latest developments and give an outlook on the potential of intelligent technologies.

Trend #1: ML platforms

Deep learning, neural networks, and natural language processing elevated ML to new levels. Thanks to mature ML algorithms, higher processing power, and the availability of huge data sets, machines are becoming intelligent and able to process unstructured data, like pictures, text, or spoken language – often even on a superhuman level. Additionally, deep learning is now stable enough to potentially establish ML as a standard commodity across businesses worldwide. Those who are interested in tailor-made and customized solutions require a ML platform to combine ready-to-use services to create their own intelligent applications.

Trend #2: Intelligent applications

Intelligent apps automate routine tasks that take time from value-adding activities and can provide precious insights into structured and unstructured enterprise data. This helps companies to make better business decisions and increase productivity in several lines of business, like finance, HR, sales and service and more. For enterprises lacking in-house ML expertise, intelligent applications are available that allow, for example, building self-driven customer service to enhance customer experience, automating financial services by matching incoming bank statements to open receivables, or helping marketing executives maximize sponsorship ROI.

Trend #3: Conversational systems

Thanks to great strides in natural language processing, conversational AI has fundamentally changed how we interact with computers and electronic devices. Today, millions of people use intelligent interfaces to satisfy their daily consumer demands. They serve users with music selections, vacation planning, pizza ordering, and much more. We are on the cusp of a world where conversational assistants will be retrievable at any time and place – including at work. These capabilities will connect data, processes, applications, devices, and people and will build the foundation for a new digital experience in the workplace.

What will the future bring us?

Technologies augmenting the human potential at work are no longer dreams of the future. But how will they evolve, and what will the trends in 2018 look like? I believe that some of these technologies might be about to reach maturity, but there is still a great deal of innovation potential, especially in the enterprise field. According to Gartner, 59% of organizations are still gathering information to start building an AI strategy for their organization – a huge competitive advantage in 2018 for those who have already started to adopt AI in their systems. I am convinced that more and more companies will leave the concept stages this year and really begin to apply ML. The hype around deep learning will flatten out as it becomes a commodity, but the efficiency and robustness of the underlying models will be the differentiator and therefore a relevant issue for enterprises to address in the upcoming year.

For Gartner, a rock-solid ML foundation, intelligent apps, and conversational platforms will make the difference between profit and loss for companies in the race to digital transformation in 2018. Platforms and solutions will evolve significantly, handling increasingly complex tasks. Further, Gartner predicts that over the next few years, every application will contain AI, creating an intelligent layer between employees and enterprise systems.

Overall, technology will become even more human-centric and will increase transparency between people, organizations, and things. In business and private life, augmented reality, virtual reality, or brain-computer interfaces will create immersive experiences beyond virtual assistants and chatbots.

Moreover, business will experience a shift from standalone intelligent objects to swarm AI – an approach that goes back to the behavior of animals that amplify their group intelligence to solve problems or make decisions. Swarm AI is the self-organization of systems for collective decentralized behavior that enables human swarms by bringing information of diverse groups into a single emergent intelligence. In an enterprise context, swarm AI helps to improve logistics or transportation, HR, or customer feedback gathering – for example, by eradicating the influence of preceding valuations on the voter. All of these AI developments will have an impact on the way enterprises are doing business, and not only on an operational level. I expect the emergence of new, AI-driven business models and a transition of innovation and research expertise, everywhere from universities to industries.

Mobility is not restricted to moving people or physical assets from A to B. Mobility is about connecting people and assets – things – and ideas, events, objects, locations, and data. Connectivity needs to be managed in a way that fulfills one task: putting digital at the service of the analog.

Mark Zuckerberg asked: "Is connectivity a human right?" Of course it is. It enables us to make use of the technological and technical progress, which is mainly driven by data and information processing. Connectivity is a human right because: "Everyone has the right of freedom to expression. This shall include freedom to hold opinions and impart information and ideas without interference by public authority and regardless of frontiers…. "(European Convention on Human Rights – Art. 10)

This means that public bodies have the obligation to provide the framework to build and extend the necessary infrastructure (i.e., 5G networks, public WiFi, LoRa, etc.), including the necessary legal framework. The challenge is that public bodies make decisions based on political expectations and interests rather than on real understanding of technical facts and evidence-based policy requirements. However, self-developing ecosystems (see cryptocurrency, shared economy, 3D printing, etc.) do not ask public authorities whether they can work or what directions to go. They just do it.

Many of these self-developing ecosystems happen in medium to large cities where academia, non-governmental organizations (NGOs), utilities, transportation companies, startups, and municipal government leaders foster the power of connectivity.

Mobile connectivity can, with the right support by governments, NGOs, academia, companies, and international bodies (like the UN), and help the human race address a lot of today's challenges such as:

- Access to education and healthcare

- Fight against hunger and poverty
- Better use of natural resources, instead of just consuming them
- Improvements that make travel more convenient and safe

With over 50% of humans living in cities, the impacts of these improvements are amplified in urban environments.

Drawbacks

We have not fully explored the ethical impacts of a connected world. AI will soon be stronger than many of us expect. AI is poised to become a full part of the connected world and needs to be designed with societies interested in mind. The same is true with nanotechnologies or biological progress (e.g., transplanted organs grown from the patient's own stem cells, CRISPR/CAS, etc.)

We need to ensure that security of connectivity is built-in by design. We still face security issues with various IoT interface protocols, for everything from traffic signals to transport management to the telecom networks that are the backbone of smart cities. This is an essential element of making connectivity useful for society.

All new devices, apps, data lakes, and other technologies must be made by design to serve the people. They must enable participation by and accept people with different attitudes, backgrounds, cognition, and cultures. Today's standardization might be efficient for some, but it should be at the service of connecting people and their individuality, supporting exponential growth of knowledge, and improving life in cities and beyond.

EMBRACING DIGITAL TRANSFORMATION: THE FUTURE OF BANKING

The face of the banking industry has changed in the last few years.

Financial technology companies (fintechs) have begun disrupting the market with cryptocurrency, bitcoin, blockchain, and more. In the United Kingdom, a new breed of banks called "challenger banks" have emerged, focusing on delivering digital-only services and exceptional customer interactions. In the United Kingdom alone, there are currently more than 20 challenger banks.

Forward-thinking banks have responded to these market disruptions by expanding their in-house capabilities. Others have partnered with fintechs to develop new digital offerings. And some simply purchased their competitors.

Banking goes digital

Digital transformation looks different in every industry and every company. In general terms, it is the integration of digital technology into all areas of a business. That integration leads to fundamental changes in how the business operates and delivers value to its customers.

Banks running on a digital core can see reduced costs and streamlined processes. This end-to-end integration also helps provide a more engaging customer experience. And it makes room for further business transformation with new digital technologies like blockchain and artificial intelligence.

Going digital has also affected the banking workforce, with automation sometimes resulting in layoffs and staff reductions. But there is a growing demand for data scientists with banking experience—a skill set not easy to find in today's market. It is time for the industry to develop a new workforce model to educate existing staff and recruit new talent.

Big Data and its impact on the customer journey

The banking industry is among the most data-driven of industries. Regulatory and insurance requirements mean banks must store many years of transaction data. The challenge is knowing how to translate that information into meaningful insights.

Big Data provides significant opportunities for banks to outshine their competition. Moving data onto a cloud platform provides a 360-degree view of every customer. This deep insight shows banks where they can provide a higher level of service and create more value. Big Data also allows the use of disruptive technologies like artificial intelligence, blockchain, and IoT to map the customer journey and gain a competitive edge.

Leveraging technology to reinvent the banking business model

New advanced technologies allow banks to strengthen customer engagement with personalized, innovative offerings. The industry already leverages IoT with mobile apps, swipe cards, ATMs, card readers, and sensors. It also provides a new opportunity for real-time asset financing.

Some banks are already using blockchain technology to transform their business processes, as it offers secure, convenient alternatives to traditional bank processes. Lately, blockchain has been in the spotlight because of its ability to reduce fraud in the financial world. Blockchain is already used in the financial instruments areas of banking, including payments (cross-border, peer-to-peer, corporate and interbank); private equity asset transfers; tracking derivative commodities; the management of trading, spending, mortgage and loan records, microfinance applications, and customer service records.

Looking at cross-border payments, for example, blockchain can be used to reduce processing time to minutes from standard times of three to six days. This elevates the customer experience to a new level with lower real-time transactions costs. Stack processes improved by blockchain include clearing networks; international transfers; clearing and settlement; auditing, reconciliation, and reporting; and asset ownership.

Banking on the cloud

Banks are racing to take advantage of market opportunities available through digital transformation. At the same time, they must manage the risks created by the new digital economy. There is a critical need for affordable computing platforms that provide greater agility.

There is no doubt that new digital technologies are changing the banking industry. Banks that embrace innovation and adopt new technologies have unprecedented opportunities to change and improve how they provide financial services including offering the ability to:

- Collaborate with financial technology partners to develop digital products.
- Provide customers with seamless real-time, multichannel digital interactions.

- Simplify and optimize business processes through standardization, optimization, and adoption of cloud solutions.
- Build an open and agile platform that makes it easy to meet regulatory requirements.
- Innovate with disruptive technologies like artificial intelligence (AI), IoT, and blockchain.

Restructuring the business model and processes is critical to any bank's successful digitalization. Leveraging innovative capabilities in a cloud deployment can not only speed up digital transformation initiatives but also deliver business-wide process improvements as well.

THE BLOCKCHAIN SOLUTION

In 2013, several UK supermarket chains discovered that products they were selling as beef were actually made at least partly—and in some cases, entirely—from horsemeat. The resulting uproar led to a series of product recalls, prompted stricter food testing, and spurred the European food industry to take a closer look at how unlabeled or mislabeled ingredients were finding their way into the food chain.

By 2020, a scandal like this will be eminently preventable.

The separation between bovine and equine will become immutable with Internet of Things (IoT) sensors, which will track the provenance and identity of every animal from stall to store, adding the data to a blockchain that anyone can check but no one can alter.

Food processing companies will be able to use that blockchain to confirm and label the contents of their products accordingly—down to the specific farms and animals represented in every individual package. That level of detail may be too much information for shoppers, but they will at least be able to trust that their meatballs come from the appropriate species.

The Spine of Digitalization

Keeping food safer and more traceable is just the beginning, however. Improvements in the supply chain, which have been incremental for decades despite billions of dollars of technology investments, are about to go exponential. Emerging technologies are converging to transform the supply chain from tactical to strategic, from an easily replicable commodity to a new source of competitive differentiation.

You may already be thinking about how to take advantage of blockchain technology, which makes data and transactions immutable, transparent, and verifiable. That will be a powerful tool to boost supply chain speed and efficiency—always a worthy goal, but hardly a disruptive one.

However, if you think of blockchain as the spine of digitalization and technologies such as AI, the IoT, 3D printing, autonomous vehicles, and drones as the limbs, you have a powerful supply chain body that can jump ahead of its competition.

In the mid-1990s, when the World Wide Web was in its infancy, we had no idea that the internet would become so large and pervasive, nor that we'd find a way to carry it all in our pockets on small slabs of glass.

But we could tell that it had vast potential.

Today, with the combination of emerging technologies that promise to turbocharge digital transformation, we're just beginning to see how we might turn the supply chain into a source of competitive advantage.

Amazon, for example, is becoming as much a logistics company as a retailer. Its ordering and delivery systems are so streamlined that its customers can launch and complete a same-day transaction with a push of a single IP-enabled button or a word to its ever-attentive AI device, Alexa. And this level of experimentation and innovation is bubbling up across industries.

Consider manufacturing, where the IoT is transforming automation inside already highly automated factories. Machine-to-machine communication is enabling robots to set up, provision, and unload equipment quickly and accurately with minimal human intervention. Meanwhile, sensors across the factory floor are already capable of gathering such information as how often each machine needs maintenance or how much raw material to order given current production trends.

Once they harvest enough data, businesses will be able to feed it through machine learning algorithms to identify trends that forecast future outcomes. At that point, the supply chain will start to become both automated and predictive. We'll begin to see business models that include proactively scheduling maintenance, replacing parts just before they're likely to break, and automatically ordering materials and initiating customer shipments.

Italian train operator Trenitalia, for example, has put IoT sensors on its locomotives and passenger cars and is using analytics and in-memory computing to gauge the health of its trains in real time, according to an information in Computer Weekly. "It is now possible to affordably collect huge amounts of data from hundreds of sensors in a single train, analyse that data in real time and detect problems before they actually happen," Trenitalia's CIO Danilo Gismondi told Computer Weekly.

Blockchain allows all the critical steps of the supply chain to go electronic and become irrefutably verifiable by all the critical parties within minutes: the seller and buyer, banks, logistics carriers, and import and export officials.

The project, which is scheduled to be completed in 2018, will change Trenitalia's business model, allowing it to schedule more trips and make each one more profitable. The railway company will be able to better plan parts inventories and determine which lines are consistently performing poorly and need upgrades. The new system will save €100 million a year, according to ARC Advisory Group.

New business models continue to evolve as 3D printers become more sophisticated and affordable, making it possible to move the end of the supply chain closer to the customer. Companies can design parts and products in materials ranging from carbon fiber to chocolate and then print those items in their warehouse, at a conveniently located third-party vendor, or even on the client's premises.

In addition to minimize their shipping expenses and reducing fulfillment time, companies will be able to offer more personalized or customized items affordably in small quantities. For example, clothing retailer Ministry of Supply recently installed a 3D printer at its Boston store that enables it to make an information of clothing to a customer's specifications in under 90 minutes, according to an information in Forbes.

This kind of highly distributed manufacturing has potential across many industries. It could even create a market for secure manufacturing for highly regulated sectors, allowing a manufacturer to transmit encrypted templates to printers in tightly protected locations, for example.

Meanwhile, organizations are investigating ways of using blockchain technology to authenticate, track and trace, automate, and otherwise manage transactions and interactions, both internally and within their vendor and customer networks. The ability to collect data, record it on the blockchain for immediate verification, and make that trustworthy data available for any application delivers indisputable value in any business context. The supply chain will be no exception.

BLOCKCHAIN IS THE CHANGE DRIVER

The supply chain is configured as we know it today because it's impossible to create a contract that accounts for every possible contingency. Consider cross-border financial transfers, which are so complex and must meet so many regulations that they require a tremendous number of intermediaries to plug the gaps: lawyers, accountants, customer service reps, warehouse operators, bankers, and more. By reducing that complexity, blockchain technology makes intermediaries less necessary—a transformation that is revolutionary even when measured only in cost savings.

"If you're selling 100 items a minute, 24 hours a day, reducing the cost of the supply chain by just $1 per item saves you more than $52.5 million a year," notes Dirk Lonser, SAP go-to-market leader at DXC Technology, an IT services company. "By replacing manual processes and multiple peer-to-peer connections through fax or e-mail with a single medium where everyone can exchange verified information instantaneously, blockchain will boost profit margins exponentially without raising prices or even increasing individual productivity."

But the potential for blockchain extends far beyond cost cutting and streamlining, says Irfan Khan, CEO of supply chain management consulting and systems integration firm Bristlecone, a Mahindra Group company. It will give companies ways to differentiate.

"Blockchain will let enterprises more accurately trace faulty parts or products from end users back to factories for recalls," Khan says. "It will streamline supplier onboarding, contracting, and management by creating an integrated platform that the company's entire network can access in real time. It will give vendors secure, transparent visibility into inventory 24/7. And at a time when counterfeiting is a real concern in multiple industries, it will make it easy for both retailers and customers to check product authenticity."

Blockchain allows all the critical steps of the supply chain to go electronic and become irrefutably verifiable by all the critical parties within minutes: the seller and buyer, banks, logistics carriers, and import and export officials. Although the key parts of the process remain the same as in today's analog supply chain, performing them electronically with blockchain technology shortens each stage from hours or days to seconds while eliminating reams of wasteful paperwork. With goods moving that quickly, companies have ample room for designing new business models around manufacturing, service, and delivery.

Challenges on the Path to Adoption

For all this to work, however, the data on the blockchain must be correct from the beginning. The pills, produce, or parts on the delivery truck need to be the same as the items listed on the manifest at the loading dock. Every use case assumes that the data is accurate—and that will only happen when everything that's manufactured is smart, connected, and able to self-verify automatically with the help of machine learning tuned to detect errors and potential fraud.

Companies are already seeing the possibilities of applying this bundle of emerging technologies to the supply chain. IDC projects that by 2021, at least 25% of Forbes Global 2000 (G2000) companies will use blockchain services as a foundation for digital trust at scale; 30% of top global manufacturers and retailers will do so by 2020. IDC also predicts that by 2020, up to 10% of pilot and production blockchain-distributed ledgers will incorporate data from IoT sensors.

Despite IDC's optimism, though, the biggest barrier to adoption is the early stage level of enterprise use cases, particularly around blockchain. Currently, the sole significant enterprise blockchain production system is the virtual currency Bitcoin, which has unfortunately been tainted by its associations with speculation, dubious financial transactions, and the so-called dark web.

The technology is still in a sufficiently early stage that there's significant uncertainty about its ability to handle the massive amounts of data a global enterprise supply chain generates daily. Never mind that it's completely unregulated, with no global standard. There's also a critical global shortage of experts who can explain emerging technologies like blockchain, the IoT, and machine learning to nontechnology industries and educate organizations in how the technologies can improve their supply chain processes. Finally, there is concern about how blockchain's complex algorithms gobble computing power—and electricity.

"We don't know yet what the market will adopt. In a decade, it might be status quo or best practice, or it could be the next Betamax, a great technology for which there was no demand," Lonser says. "Even highly regulated industries that need greater transparency in the entire supply chain are moving fairly slowly."

Blockchain will require acceptance by a critical mass of companies, governments, and other organizations before it displaces paper documentation. It's a chicken-and-egg issue: multiple companies need to adopt these technologies at the same time so they can build a blockchain to exchange information, yet getting multiple companies to do anything simultaneously is a challenge. Some early initiatives are already underway, though:

- A London-based startup called Everledger is using blockchain and IoT technology to track the provenance, ownership, and lifecycles of valuable assets. The company began by tracking diamonds using roughly 200 different characteristics, with a goal of stopping both the demand for and the supply of "conflict diamonds"—diamonds mined in war zones and sold to finance insurgencies. It has since than expanded to cover wine, artwork, and other high-value items to prevent fraud and verify authenticity.

• In September 2017, SAP announced the creation of its SAP Leonardo Blockchain Co-Innovation program, a group of 27 enterprise customers interested in co-innovating around blockchain and creating business buy-in. The diverse group of participants includes management and technology services companies Capgemini and Deloitte, cosmetics company Natura Cosméticos S.A., and Moog Inc., a manufacturer of precision motion control systems.

• Two of Europe's largest shipping ports— Rotterdam and Antwerp—are working on blockchain projects to streamline interaction with port customers. The Antwerp terminal authority says eliminating paperwork could cut the costs of container transport by as much as 50%.

• The Chinese online retailer Alibaba is experimenting blockchain to verify the authenticity of food products and catch counterfeits before they endanger people's health and lives.

• Technology and transportation executives have teamed up to create the Blockchain in Transport Alliance (BiTA), a forum for developing blockchain standards and education for the freight industry.

It's likely that the first blockchain-based enterprise supply chain use case will emerge in the next year among companies that see it as an opportunity to bolster their legal compliance and improve business processes. Once that happens, expect others to follow.

Customers Will Expect Change

It's only a matter of time before the supply chain becomes a competitive driver. The question for today's enterprises is how to prepare for the shift. Customers are going to expect constant, granular visibility into their transactions and faster, more customized service every step of the way. Organizations will need to be ready to meet those expectations.

If organizations have manual business processes that could never be automated before, now is the time to see if it's possible. Organizations that have made initial investments in emerging technologies are looking at how their pilot projects are paying off and where they might extend to the supply chain. They are starting to think creatively about how to combine technologies to offer a product, service, or business model not possible before.

A manufacturer will load a self-driving truck with a 3D printer capable of creating a customer's ordered item en route to delivering it. A vendor will capture the market for a socially responsible product by allowing its customers to track the product's production and verify that none of its subcontractors use slave labor. And a supermarket chain will win over customers by persuading them that their choice of supermarket is also a choice between being certain of what's in their food and simply hoping that what's on the label matches what's inside.

Over the past few years, technology has seen a significant shift from cyclical, invention-led spending on point solutions to investments targeting customer-driven, end-to-end value. The next wave of disruption and productivity improvements is here, which means a huge opportunity for digital-focused enterprises – if you are following the right roadmap.

Technology trends have significant potential over the next few years. Establishing a digital platform will not only set the stage for business innovation to provide competitive advantage, but it will also create new business models that will change the way we do business. Technology trends in 2018 will lay the foundation for the maturity of innovative technologies like artificial intelligence and machine learning and will prepare both businesses and shoppers to be ready for their consumption.

Like any other industry, retail is being disrupted. It is no longer enough to simply stock racks with alluring products and wait for customers to rush through the door. Technological innovation is changing the way we shop. Customers can find the lowest price for any product with just a few screen touches. They can read online reviews, have products sent to their home, try them, and return anything they don't want – all for little or nothing out of pocket. If there are problems, they can use social networks to call out brands that come up short.

Retailers are making their products accessible from websites and mobile applications, with many running effective Internet business operations rather than brick-and-mortar stores. They convey merchandise to the customer's front entry and are set up with web-based networking media if things turn out badly.

Smart retailers are striving to fulfill changing customer needs and working to guarantee top customer service regardless of how their customer interacts with them.

2017 saw the development of some progressive technology in retail, and 2018 will be another energizing year for the retail industry. Today's informed customers expect a more engaging shopping experience, with a consistent mix of both online and in-store recommendations. The retail experience is poised to prosper throughout next couple of years – for retailers that are prepared to embrace technology.

Here are four areas of retail technology I predict will take off in 2018:

In-store GPS-driven shopping trolleys

Supermarkets like Tesco and Sainsbury's now enable their customers to scan and pay for products using a mobile app instead of waiting in a checkout line. The next phase of this involves intelligent shopping trolleys, or grocery store GPS: Customers use a touch screen to load shopping lists, and the system helps them find the items in the store. Customers can then check off and pay for items as they go, directly on-screen. These shopping trolleys will make their way into stores around the last quarter of 2018.

Electronic rack edge names

Electronic rack edge names are not yet broadly utilized, but this could change in 2018 as more retailers adopt this technology. Currently, retail workers must physically select and update printed labels to reflect changes in price, promotions, etc. This technology makes the process more efficient by handling such changes electronically.

Reference point technology

Despite the fact that it's been around since 2013, reference point technology hasn't yet been utilized to its fullest potential. In the last few years, however, it's started to pick up in industries like retail. It's now being used by a few retailers for area-based promotions.

Some interesting uses I've observed: Retailers can send messages to customers when they're nearby a store location, and in-store mannequins can offer information about the clothing and accessories they're wearing. I anticipate that this innovation will take off throughout 2018 and into 2019.

Machine intelligence

The technological innovations describe above will also provide retailers with new data streams. These data sources, when merged with existing customer data, online, and ERP data, will lead to new opportunities. Recently Walmart announced it would begin utilizing rack examining robots to help review its stores. The machines will check stock, prices, and even help settle lost inventory. It will also help retailers learn more about changing customer behavior in real time, which will boost engagement.

Clearly, technology and digital transformation in retail have changed the way we live and shop. 2018 will see emerging technologies like machine learning and artificial intelligence using structured and unstructured data to deliver innovation. As technology develops, it will continue to transform and enhance the retail experience.

By creating user interfaces which let us work with the representations inside machine learning models, we can give people new tools for reasoning.

What are computers for?

Historically, there are different answers to this question, different visions of computing, have helped inspire and determine the computing systems that humanity has ultimately built. Consider the early electronic computers. ENIAC, the world's first general-purpose electronic computer, was commissioned to compute artillery firing tables for the United States Army. Other early computers were also used to solve numerical problems, such as simulating nuclear explosions, predicting the weather,

58

and planning the motion of rockets. The machines operated in a batch mode, using crude input and output devices, and without any real-time interaction. It was a vision of computers as number-crunching machines, used to speed up calculations that would formerly have taken weeks, months, or more for a team of humans.

In the 1950s a different vision of what computers are for began to develop. That vision was crystallized in 1962, when Douglas Engelbart proposed that computers could be used as a way of augmenting human intellect.

In this view, computers weren't primarily tools for solving number-crunching problems. Rather, they were real-time interactive systems, with rich inputs and outputs, that humans could work with to support and expand their own problem-solving process. This vision of intelligence augmentation (IA) deeply influenced many others, including researchers such as Alan Kay at Xerox PARC, entrepreneurs such as Steve Jobs at Apple, and led to many of the key ideas of modern computing systems. Its ideas have also deeply influenced digital art and music, and fields such as interaction design, data visualization, computational creativity, and human-computer interaction.

Research on IA has often been in competition with research on artificial intelligence (AI): competition for funding, and for the interest of talented researchers. Although there has always been overlap between the fields, IA has typically focused on building systems which put humans and machines to work together, while AI has focused on complete outsourcing of intellectual tasks to machines. In particular, problems in AI are often framed in terms of matching or surpassing human performance: beating humans at chess or Go; learning to recognize speech and images or translating language as well as humans; and so on.

This essay describes a new field, emerging today out of a synthesis of AI and IA. For this field, we suggest the name artificial intelligence augmentation (AIA): the use of AI systems to help develop new methods for intelligence augmentation. This new field introduces important new fundamental questions, questions not associated to either parent field. We believe the principles and systems of AIA will be radically different to most existing systems.

Our essay begins with a survey of recent technical work hinting at artificial intelligence augmentation, including work on generative interfaces – that is, interfaces which can be used to explore and visualize generative machine learning models. Such interfaces develop a kind of cartography of generative models, ways for humans to explore and make meaning from those models, and to incorporate what those models "know" into their creative work.

This essay is not just a survey of technical work. We believe now is a good time to identify some of the broad, fundamental questions at the foundation of this emerging field. To what extent are these new tools enabling creativity? Can they be used to generate ideas which are truly surprising and new, or are the ideas cliches, based on trivial recombination of existing ideas? Can such systems be used to develop fundamental new interface primitives? How will those new primitives change and expand the way humans think?

Using generative models to invent meaningful creative operations

Let's look at an example where a machine learning model makes a new type of interface possible. To understand the interface, imagine you're a type designer, working on creating a new font 1 . After sketching some initial designs, you wish to experiment with bold, italic, and condensed variations. Let's examine a tool to generate and explore such variations, from any initial design. For reasons that will soon be explained the quality of results is quite crude; please bear with us.

Of course, varying the bolding (i.e., the weight), italicization and width are just three ways you can vary a font. Imagine that instead of building specialized tools, users could build their own tool merely by choosing examples of existing fonts. For instance, suppose you wanted to vary the degree of serifing on a font. In the following, please select 5 to

10 sans-serif fonts from the top box, and drag them to the box on the left. Select 5 to 10 serif fonts and drag them to the box on the right. As you do this, the machine learning model running in your browser will automatically infer from these examples, how to interpolate your starting font in either the serif or sans-serif direction:

In fact, we used this same technique to build the earlier bolding italicization, and condensing tool. To do so, we used the following examples of bold and non-bold fonts, of italic and non-italic fonts, and of condensed and non-condensed fonts:

BOLD

ITALIC

CONDENSED

'LEARN WITH GOOGLE AI' IS A MACHINE LEARNING COURSE, WHICH IS FREE AND OPEN TO ALL

Google's "Learn with Google AI" is a new course introduced by the company, which will bring machine learning skills and concepts to all users who sign up. The course is free and available to all who are interested. Google says the set of educational resources in this course have been developed by machine learning experts at the company. Google says also that the idea with this machine learning course, is to encourage people to learn about machine learning concepts, developping skills in the area, and applying artificial intelligence to real-world problems.

The new Machine Learning Crash Course will give a quick introduction to practical ML concepts using high-level TensorFlow (TF) APIs. TensorFlow is Google's open source library for machine learning tools and can be accessed by anyone to build AI, ML frameworks suited to their problems. Machine Learning allows computers to learn, understand and recognise the data, without being explicitly programmed to do so. Machine Learning is the building block for artificial intelligence and is what powers self-driving cars, image recognition, etc. Google products like Google Photos, Google Translate, Google Assistant, etc all rely on an aspect of machine learning to carry out some tasks.

Google AI is making it easier for everyone to learn ML by providing a huge range of free, in-depth educational content. This is for everyone — from deep ML experts looking for advanced developer tutorials and materials, to curious people who are ready to try to learn what ML is in the first place," Zuri Kemp, Program Manager for Google's machine learning education said in a press statement.

How to enroll for Google Machine Learning course? What are the requirements?

Those who are interested can access the Google Machine Learning course at developers.google.com/machine-learning/crash-course/. While the course is free for all, there are some pre-requisites before taking up an understanding of how to code for machine learning. Google's course page says a mastery of introductory level of algebra is a must for those who wish to sign up for this course. This includes understanding of variables and coefficients, linear equations, graphs of functions, and histograms. Also familiarity with advanced math concepts such as logarithms and derivatives will be helpful, though it is not compulsory.

Additionally is required a basic knowledge of programming, and some experience coding in Python are also required. Google says those enrolling should be comfortable reading and writing Python code since the exercises in the course in the same programming language. The course will have lectures from Google's AI experts, along with exercises and access to some material as well.

The Google course on Machine Learning was originally built for the company's own employees and so far over 18,000 employees in the company have enrolled in this MLCC course. Google says that seeing the program's success in-house is what inspired them to make it available to everyone.

Despite radical advances in technology, many companies still plan routes for their delivery trucks the same way they did a decade ago. Managers create itineraries the day before, and then hand printouts to drivers to follow or add them to the hand-held devices that their drivers carry at their hip.

But when drivers get stuck in traffic jams while on their rounds, they're simply out of luck and behind schedule. The same thing happens if there's a surprise snowstorm that makes roads impassable.

In short, the routes are inflexible.

But there is an IA that track this age-old problem by pairing machine learning with data it collects from drivers' mobile phones. It crunches information like the driver's speed and GPS location with other details including traffic, weather, where the order is being delivered, and when customers are available to receive their orders.

What emerges is a delivery route that can be tweaked on the fly depending on any complications that come up. If the technology determines that a driver will miss a scheduled stop because of road closures, for example, it will adjust the schedule for the entire day. If that's not possible, the driver will receive alerts on his or her mobile phone as a not-so subtle hint to pick up the pace. (Red is not a good sign.)

The goal is to create routes that allow drivers to work more efficiently. By doing so, companies can save money by increasing the number of deliveries that drivers can make during shifts while also making customers happier by improving the likelihood that orders will arrive on time, or by the driver they prefer.

Optimizing delivery routes has its roots in what's called the Traveling Salesman Problem, which mathematicians have been trying to solve since 1930. While the task is straightforward—finding most efficient route between cities for salesmen before returning home—it remains unsolved. The possibilities are limitless, much like the possibilities for deliveries.

The algorithms learn from each day's data so that it can improve the routes the technology provides going forward.

Increasing the efficiency of deliveries is now more important than ever for companies as they battle for customers who expect their orders almost immediately. Amazon, for example, offers same-day deliveries of groceries and certain Prime products within one- and two-hour delivery windows, requiring huge computing power and machine learning tools.

But creating such a system is difficult. UPS has been building its own custom software—Orion—for over a decade. Over 500 people reportedly worked on the technology, but after 10 years, it's still not fully deployed. In Manhattan, UPS drivers still use an old version called ED because Orion doesn't do well in complex urban environments.

For over 20 years, Anheuser-Busch used Roadnet, a technology that creates delivery routes up to the day of. Roadnet helps build the plan and set the sequence, but those routes don't change after drivers get on the road.

Another problem became apparent when Anheuser-Busch compared the routes the Roadnet software created with those that drivers actually took. The company found that drivers often deviated from the plan. It was a sign that drivers thought they knew better than the technology, an easy slip-up when they follow the same route every day for years. It also highlighted the problem of incorporating some of the on-the-job knowledge that drivers had about their routes that technology has difficulty capturing.

In urban markets where employees are trained to use these tools properly, Anheuser-Busch says it has reduced the miles traveled per stop by 4%, which translates into fuel savings, lower wear and tear on trucks, and, for the driver, improved earnings based on higher productivity.

VIRTUAL CELL CAN SIMULATE CELLULAR GROWTH USING MACHINE LEARNING

Scientists have created a virtual yeast cell model that can learn from real-world behaviors, a key step in utilizing artificial intelligence in healthcare to diagnose diseases.

A team of researchers from the University of California San Diego has developed what they called a "visible" neural network that enabled them to build DCell—a machine learning model of a functioning brewer's yeast cell that is commonly used in basic research.

Machine learning systems are built on a neural network that consist of layers of artificial neurons that are tied together by seemingly random connections between neurons. The systems "learn" by fine-tuning those connections.

In DCell, the researchers amassed all knowledge of cell biology in one place and created a hierarchy of the cellular components.

DCell's learning is guided by real-world cellular behaviors and constraints, coded from approximately 2,500 known cellular components. The researchers input information about genes and genetic mutation, allowing the system to predict cellular behaviors like growth. DCell, which is trained on several million genotypes, found that the virtual cell could simulate cellular growth nearly as accurately as a real cell grown in a laboratory.

"Human knowledge is incomplete," said Jianzhu Ma, PhD, an assistant research scientist who led the efforts to build DCell, said in a statement. "We want to complete that knowledge to help guide predictions, in health care and elsewhere."

The researchers tested the new system by deliberately feeding it false information. The system was able to decipher that it was false information and refused to work.

When the researchers wired ribosomes to an unrelated process like apoptosis, DCell could no longer predict cell growth. The virtual cell "knows" that the new arrangement is not biologically possible.

The research team is now generating some of the experimental data they would need to build a DCell system for cancer and determine how to best personalize the virtual cell approach for each individual patient's unique biology.

A VISUAL INTRODUCTION TO MACHINE LEARNING

In machine learning, computers apply statistical learning techniques to automatically identify patterns in data. These techniques can be used to make highly accurate predictions.

Keep scrolling. Using a data set about homes, we will create a machine learning model to distinguish homes in New York from homes in San Francisco.

Let's say you had to determine whether a home is in San Francisco or in New York. In machine learning terms, categorizing data points is a classification task.

Since San Francisco is relatively hilly, the elevation of a home may be a good way to distinguish the two cities.

Based on the home-elevation data to the right, you could argue that a home above 73 meters should be classified as one in San Francisco.

Adding nuance

Adding another dimension allows for more nuance. For example, New York apartments can be extremely expensive per square foot.

So visualizing elevation and price per square foot in a scatterplot helps us distinguish lower-elevation homes.

The data suggests that, among homes at or below 73 meters, those that cost more than $19,116.7 per square meter are in New York City.

Dimensions in a data set are called features, predictors, or variables.

Drawing boundaries

You can visualize your elevation (>73 m) and price per square foot (>$19,116.7) observations as the boundaries of regions in your scatterplot. Homes plotted in the green and blue regions would be in San Francisco and New York, respectively.

Identifying boundaries in data using math is the essence of statistical learning.

Of course, you'll need additional information to distinguish homes with lower elevations and lower per-square-foot prices.

The dataset we are using to create the model has 7 different dimensions. Creating a model is also known as training a model.

On the right, we are visualizing the variables in a scatterplot matrix to show the relationships between each pair of dimensions.

There are clearly patterns in the data, but the boundaries for delineating them are not obvious.

And now, machine learning

Finding patterns in data is where machine learning comes in. Machine learning methods use statistical learning to identify boundaries.

One example of a machine learning method is a decision tree. Decision trees look at one variable at a time and are a reasonably accessible (though rudimentary) machine learning method.

CONCLUSION

Machine-learning algorithms are used on smaller-screen devices. As the technology expands, more and more memory as well as battery power is needed to perform the processing. As a result, data has to be transferred to a server to allow the operation of the algorithms. The system is always deleting older data so there is enough storage space.

Machine Learning

A Guide For Beginner

Leonard Eddison

Respective authors own all copyrights not held by the publisher.

The information herein is offered for informational purposes solely, and is universal as so. The presentation of the information is without contract or any type of guarantee assurance.

The trademarks that are used are without any consent, and the publication of the trademark is without permission or backing by the trademark owner. All trademarks and brands within this book are for clarifying purposes only and are the owned by the owners themselves, not affiliated with this document.

Page intentionally left blank

INTRODUCTION

MACHINE LEARNING AN IT ESSENTIAL

A machine learning business could very well be your best opportunity as an IT professional. That's because this unique area of the computer world is one that requires a great deal of specialized skill to navigate while at the same time being an essential part of much consumer computer activity. In other words, it's necessary but there are only few people who can do it.

Not surprisingly, you can see how being able to bridge the gap and allowing companies to make use of machine learning to drive their business would make your services extremely valuable. That's why, if you're looking to start an online internet business and you have the necessary knowledge, then machine learning could be the perfect field for you.

So what exactly is machine learning and why is it so valuable in the online business world? Simply put, it is a method of data analysis that uses algorithms that learn from data and produce specific results without being specifically programmed to do so. These algorithms can analyze data, calculate how frequently certain parts of it are used and generate responses based on these calculations in order to automatically interact with users.

In fact, machine learning is used in a number of capacities in today's world, from generating those "other items you may be interested in" responses at sites like Amazon, to providing fraud detection, to generating web search results and filtering spam in e-mail servers. These are just a few of the common applications of this process, all of which can be extremely important to companies for driving business.

By using machine learning, companies can personalize their customer's experience, make sure that the right products are being put in front of them at the right time and make sure that their company is coming up in web searches to reach the largest possible audience of potential customers. With your own machine learning business, you can step in and help them to achieve these ends.

The one common factor in all of the applications of machine learning is that while the connection from point A to point B may seem obvious, actually getting there can be like reading ancient Greek. If you don't know what you're looking at, you won't be able to get very far. So companies will be all too eager to employ someone who can find their way through this thorny path and get the results they want.

By playing up how you can use machine learning to help their company and positioning yourself as the best possible option for handling this end of business technology, you'll be creating a tremendous money making opportunity for yourself. And nothing can keep that business going better than a host of satisfied customers ready to spread the word about your quality services.

Gaining a foothold in the ever expanding IT field can be daunting, but it can be done if you go about it the right way. One important factor is choosing the right areas to concentrate on. If you have the skills and knowledge to handle it, then opening a machine learning business may just be your best bet for guaranteed success.

CHAPTER ONE

WHAT DOES MACHNE LEARNING MEAN ?

Machine Learning is a new trending field these days and is an application of artificial intelligence. It uses certain statistical algorithms to make computers work in a certain way without being explicitly programmed. The algorithms receive an input value and predict an output for this by the use of certain statistical methods. The main aim of machine learning is to create intelligent machines which can think and work like human beings.

REQUIREMENTS OF CREATING GOOD MACHINE LEARNING SYSTEMS

So what is required for creating such intelligent systems? Following are the things required in creating such machine learning systems:

• Data - Input data is required for predicting the output.

• Algorithms - Machine Learning is dependent on certain statistical algorithms to determine data patterns.

• Automation - It is the ability to make systems operate automatically.

• Iteration - The complete process is an iterative i.e. repetition of the process.

• Scalability - The capacity of the machine can be increased or decreased in size and scale.

• Modeling - The models are created according to the demand by the process of modeling.

Methods of Machine Learning

The methods are classified into certain categories. These are:

• Supervised Learning - In this method, input and output is provided to the computer along with feedback during the training. The accuracy of predictions by the computer during training is also analyzed. The main goal of this training is to make computers learn how to map input to the output.

• Unsupervised Learning - In this case, no such training is provided leaving computers to find the output on its own. Unsupervised learning is mostly applied on transactional data. It is used in more complex tasks. It uses another approach of iteration known as deep learning to arrive at some conclusions.

• Reinforcement Learning - This type of learning uses three components namely - agent, environment, action. An agent is the one that perceives its surroundings, an environment is the one with which an agent interacts and acts in that environment. The main goal in reinforcement learning is to find the best possible policy.

HOW DOES MACHINE LEARNING WORK?

Machine learning makes use of processes similar to that of data mining. The algorithms are described in terms of target function(f) that maps input variable (x) to an output variable (y). This can be represented as:

$y=f(x)$

There is also an error e which is the independent of the input variable x. Thus the more generalized form of the equation is:

$y=f(x) + e$

The most common type of machine learning is designed to learn the mapping of x to y for predictions.There are various assumptions for this function.

Applications of Machine Learning

The following are some of the applications:

- Cognitive Services

- Medical Services

- Language Processing

- Business Management

- Image Recognition

- Face Detection

- Video Games

BENEFITS OF MACHINE LEARNING

Everything is dependent on these systems. Find out what are the benefits of this.

- Decision making is faster - It provides the best possible outcomes by prioritizing the routine decision-making processes.

- Adaptability - It provides the ability to adapt to new changing environment rapidly. The environment changes rapidly due to the fact that data is being constantly updated.

• Innovation - It uses advanced algorithms that improve the overall decision-making capacity. This helps in developing innovative business services and models.

• Insight - It helps in understanding unique data patterns and based on which specific actions can be taken.

• Business growth - With machine learning overall business process and workflow will be faster and hence this would contribute to the overall business growth and acceleration.

• Outcome will be good - With this the quality of the outcome will be improved with lesser chances of error.

DEEP LEARNING

Deep Learning is a part of the broader field machine learning and is based on data representation learning. It is based on the interpretation of artificial neural network. Deep Learning algorithm uses many layers of processing. Each layer uses the output of previous layer as an input to itself. The algorithm used can be a supervised algorithm or an unsupervised algorithm.

Deep Neural Network

Deep Neural Network is a type of Artificial Neural Network with multiple layers which are hidden between the input layer and the output layer. This concept is known as feature hierarchy and it tends to increase the complexity and abstraction of data. This gives network the ability to handle very large, high-dimensional data sets having millions of parameters

CHAPTER TWO

MACHINE LEARNING AND ARTIFICIAL INTELLIGENCE

Artificial Intelligence is a branch of computer science which aims to create intelligence machines. This word was coined by John McCarthy in 1956 and defines it as "the science and engineering of making intelligent machines." It has been a very hot subject of breathtaking optimism which has been met with lot of setback in later years, but today it is an essential base for modern technology and solves many difficult problems in computer science.

Research in AI is an ongoing process that mainly include reasoning, planning, communication, learning, perception, knowledge and the ability to move and manipulate objects. There are so many theoretical difference of opinion, many researches no longer believes that AI is possible with computers. Some believe thinking machines and AI are just myth, fiction and speculation seen only in movies and books. In mid of 20th century, research and study on AI were on the main stream of computer science development. Few scientist began the research to build intelligent machines based on neurology. They also started their research on a new mathematical theory of information, with control and stability mechanisms called cybernetics, which lead to the invention of digital computer.

Artificial intelligence is now widely been used in all fields viz. robotics, medicine(diagnosis), market trading, computer games, rockets, toys, search engines and name a lot more. To be true AI is not used exactly how it was proposed to be used but only the effect of it is being used: it is the so called Artificial Intelligence effect. From the start of research of AI it has not only claimed to recreate human mind capabilities but also an inspiration for philosophy. A few are:

- Turing's "polite convention"
- Dartmouth proposal
- Newell and Simon's physical symbol system hypothesis
- Gödel's incompleteness theorem
- Searle's strong AI hypothesis
- The artificial brain argument

As the AI was a huge body the researchers split it into several different approaches and opinions with modern methods and theories to quench the thirst to create intelligent machines. They start them with two basic approaches, bottom-up and top-down. Wherein the bottom-up approach deals with AI to be built with human brain's neuron into electronic replica of it and whereas top-down approach believes computer programs to mimic brain's behaviors. These two are the main methods used to create variety of programs, as research progressed in development of AI more complex theories and methods being started to come in use and now scientists are busy building more powerful AI programs with these.

But unfortunately AI does have few problems, the major one is due to the split of the approaches to built the AI machine, the sub-fields often fails to communicate fairly with each other to make them complete. As the sub-fields develop around a particular research or say problem with different approaches and tools, it becomes hectic to combine them to give a consolidated result. So the scientist again divides these problems into sub problems to solve them and built an AI program.

Thus, AI is now become a more common and ongoing research with various sub-fields into it. It's now not long enough when we would be able to get the big product of it out in the world as our ancestors would have like to see it through.

The technology is an essential piece of the modern science and advancement in respect of empowering electronic gadgets and to perform on a scale. As we know the technology is in demand for last a decade and measure of development have been done in the earlier decade applying this technology. Most of the smart gadgets we are using today are the great result of this technology. Sometimes the advancement of this technology makes me sit and think that, is it artificial intelligence?

Machine Learning (ML) is so unavoidable nowadays that we utilize it doubtlessly by and large in a day without recognizing it. Researchers break down and continue with work to make this technology as a good source to make progress towards human-level AI.

The methods of this technology have been upgraded in 10 years prior to administer and improve the new handling advancements easily. It is rapidly making a phase and adequately accepting by the world; scholastics interested in electronic thinking and investigate to get the accomplishment if a machine could pick up from data.

Change of this innovation is basic to invigorate the master advancement if models revealed new data; they should have the ability to independently change. Everything thought of it as is imperative to make it straightforward to use in various fields. In future, it will be a basic and strong methodology to make the inert requesting in a going with way -

- Financial Trading
- Healthcare
- Marketing Personalization
- Fraud Acknowledgment
- Recommendations
- Online look for Data Monitoring
- Natural tongue taking care of
- Smart Vehicles

ML is the specialty of creating electronic gadgets to act without being unequivocally modified. In the earlier decade, the technology has given us self-driving cars, helpful talk affirmation, effective web look, and a vastly improved appreciation of the human genome. In this article, you will get some answers concerning the best of this system, and get take a shot at executing them and moving them to work for yourself.

Machine Learning: Value For Business

Machine learning (ML) algorithms allows computers to define and apply rules which were not described explicitly by the developer.

There are quite a lot of articles devoted to machine learning algorithms. Here is an attempt to make a "helicopter view" description of how these algorithms are applied in different business areas. This list is not an exhaustive list of course.

The first point is that ML algorithms can assist people by helping them to find patterns or dependencies, which are not visible by a human.

Numeric forecasting seems to be the most well known area here. For a long time computers were actively used for predicting the behavior of financial markets. Most models were developed before the 1980s, when financial markets got access to sufficient computational power. Later these technologies spread to other industries. Since computing power is cheap now, it can be used by even small companies for all kinds of forecasting, such as traffic (people, cars, users), sales forecasting and more.

Anomaly detection algorithms help people scan lots of data and identify which cases should be checked as anomalies. In finance they can identify fraudulent transactions. In infrastructure monitoring they make it possible to identify problems before they affect business. It is used in manufacturing quality control.

The main idea here is that you should not describe each type of anomaly. You give a big list of different known cases (a learning set) to the system and system use it for anomaly identifying.

Object clustering algorithms allows to group big amount of data using wide range of meaningful criteria. A man can't operate efficiently with more than few hundreds of object with many parameters. Machine can do clustering more efficient, for example, for customers / leads qualification, product lists segmentation, customer support cases classification etc.

Recommendations / preferences / behavior prediction algorithms gives us opportunity to be more efficient interacting with customers or users by offering them exactly what they need, even if they have not thought about it before. Recommendation systems works really bad in most of services now, but this sector will be improved rapidly very soon.

The second point is that machine learning algorithms can replace people. System makes analysis of people's actions, build rules basing on this information (i.e. learn from people) and apply this rules acting instead of people.

First of all this is about all types of standard decisions making. There are a lot of activities which require standard actions in standard situations. People make "standard decisions" and escalate cases which are not standard. There are no reasons, why machines can't do that: documents processing, cold calls, bookkeeping, first line customer support etc.

And again, the main feature here is that ML does not require for explicit rules definition. It "learns" from cases, which are already resolved by people during their work, and it makes the learning process cheaper. Such systems will save a lot of money for business owners, but many people will lose their job.

Another fruitful area is all kinds of data harvesting / web scraping. Google knows a lot. But when you need to get some aggregated structured information from the web, you still need to attract a human to do that (and there is a big chance that result will not be really good). Information aggregation, structuring and cross-validation, based on your preferences and requirements, will be automated thanks to ML. Qualitative analysis of information will still be made by people.

CHAPTER THREE

ADVANTAGES OF ARTIFICIAL INTELLIGENCE
APPLIED TO EVERYDAY SITUATIONS

Auto dealers are losing their battle with their customers when it comes to controlling the road to the sale. Customers have been emboldened by their access to information on the internet making them as informed as the salespeople who claim to have all the answers. The latest bump on the internet super highway, for customers, is the ability for auto dealers to apply predictive marketing messages coupled with personalized conversion tools on their websites. The salesperson has regained control of the steering wheel by answering their customers' questions before they even have to ask them.

Artificial Intelligence has gotten a bad rap starting with its name since it isn't as "artificial" as it sounds. Today's software are focused on enhancing the customer experience by providing transparency for online shoppers has an hidden power. It allows the auto dealer to monitor customer activity in their virtual showroom as well as subsequent online visits to competing dealerships or third-party sites. The data collected can then be applied to develop algorithms powering machine learning, (artificial intelligence), which can predict what the customer is really looking for. With that knowledge the dealer can deliver personalized targeted messages designed to satisfy the customers' wants and needs by offering exactly the vehicle they are looking for.

The truth is that artificial intelligence is simply the collected wisdom and experience of the human beings that write the algorithms that drives it. There is no replacement for experience. The data accumulated by machine learning powered software platforms provide the collected experiences of thousands of customers along with the trial and error attempts to sell them a vehicle resulting in the best chance to earn their business. Human nature isn't discarded by the software, it is collected and applied to their problem solving capabilities.

Software as a solution is a proven way to provide efficiencies in sales and service processes at an auto dealership by improving on the people part of the process. The secret to the next generation of artificial intelligence powered software is that the people are baked into the technical cake.

The challenge for auto dealers moving forward is to observe problems in their sales processes from their customers' perspective. Solutions that allow the customer to feel like they are in charge will be more easily accepted than anything that even the best intentioned salesperson can present.

Old school wisdom based on understanding human nature aren't replaced by software, even using artificial intelligence. They are simply enhanced with the power of technology which is the universal change agent.

Artificial Intelligence

Science fiction has built up the idea of artificial intelligence for years. Giving machines intelligence often spells the end of mankind as they then rise up against their creators and violently free themselves from oppression. There are cautionary tales such as in the film "Spider Man 2" in which the robotic arms of Dr.

Octavius start controlling his brain thus forcing him to perform actions of benefit to them.

Real AI is quite fascinating and in many ways entirely different to what I expected.

To start with, what exactly is AI

1. The ability of a computer or other machine to perform those activities that are normally thought to require intelligence.

2. The branch of computer science concerned with the development of machines having this ability.

If you take a look at this you may notice that the field of AI is actually far broader than many people give it credit for. Even the Google search engine can be said to incorporate some of the researches done in AI. The definition of AI and intelligence itself sometimes varies but it's probably safe to say that a simple explanation is that if a machine exhibits a measure of intelligence in some area it can be called AI.

The AI of movies is usually entirely self aware, emotive, and for all intents and purposes 'alive'. It is capable of learning, reasoning, explaining and deceiving. The AI I've experienced is far more specialized, focusing on just one aspect of a problem that could potentially be much larger. There are various areas of research being carried out into creating the humanoid machines of science fiction, but as yet most are still restricted to the realms of the imagination. One very impressive piece of technology is the Honda ASIMO project. This project has created a humanoid robot with some remarkable features. I'm not entirely sure if there's really a practical use for this (I think they're just trying to justify their funding with the applications mentioned on the website) but it scores points for being one of the coolest uses of technology I've ever seen.

From what I can tell ASIMO isn't intended to be a particularly human robot beyond superficial levels. He doesn't exhibit emotion or learn outside of his constraints (he can learn areas and navigate them etc. but you couldn't just sit down and teach him to play the piano without getting in and doing some serious reprogramming). He's not going to be fooling anyone into believing that he's human any time soon.

The Turing Test is a measure of Artificial Intelligence that was created by Alan Turing. He stated that the question of whether or not machines could think was too vague, and proposed a test that was more specific. His test, without going into too much detail, involved trying to get a computer to fool people into believing that it was human. The people would type a question into a console and receive a response from the computer on the other side. While there has been much work done on systems trying to pass the Turing test, none of them have succeeded yet. There has also been research done into creating machines that can exhibit emotions. However, we're still a long way off from seeing a machine that can appear to be alive.

The early excitement over AI led to developers trying to create a generic reasoning problem solver that could search through a mass of knowledge that it has acquired and find solutions to any problem that was thrown at it. Unfortunately this proved almost impossible in practice. Today's AI tends to focus on very specific problems and knowledge areas. Expert Systems are programs that are "Experts" in a specific field and can answer queries related to only that field. Their applications include medical diagnosis, credit card application, and other fields where data is to be analyzed.

CHAPTER FOUR

SOME OF THE BRANCHES OF ARTIFICIAL INTELLIGENCE

Artificial Intelligence (AI) is a branch of computer science, which tries to give "intelligence to machines". But the concept of intelligence itself is debatable, and making these machines without life "intelligent" is something near to impossible. But we can say safely that AI aims at producing intelligent behavior from machines. What is the difference between having intelligence and having intelligent behavior? You can exhibit intelligent behavior in a narrow field for some time without really being intelligent. For example a computer playing chess at the master level does not even know that it is playing chess. But for the outsider the view is that it is intelligent like a master. Also we need only this intelligent behavior for many practical purposes.

AI uses ideas from diverse branches of knowledge like computer science, economics, biology, social sciences, mathematics and even grammar. It has also diverse applications in many areas of life. That is, it is an interdisciplinary subject, which takes ideas from almost all fields of knowledge and has applications in many diverse areas of life. Some of the branches of AI are discussed below. This in no way is a complete list.

1. Game playing:

Playing a game like checkers, chess, or go, requires a lot of intelligence for a human being and so these tasks were one of the earliest attractions of AI. Samuel wrote a program playing checkers in the 60's and many people contributed to the theory of game playing. Finally when a computer could beat the then world champion in a chess game, that was considered a victory of machine over man even though it was not so.

2. Automatic theorem proving:

Mathematicians are believed to be super intelligent creatures, and so in its early childhood AI tried to show intelligence by creating machines capable of proving theorems by themselves. By having some basic assumptions and rules, they tried to prove theorems by combining these rules, getting new assumptions and so on. Gelernters program for geometry theorem proving was a typical example. Later it was realized that the intelligence of human experts in this area is not easily imitable, and the use of common sense and knowledge about mathematics was needed to prove theorems. Currently not many developments are taking place in this area.

3.Natural language processing (NLP)

Languages like English, French or Malayalam, which are used by men, are called natural languages. The language we speak is often context sensitive. "Did you shoot the tiger?" has different meanings when asked to a hunter and a photographer. Also our language is incomplete. Natural language processing deals with understanding this language using knowledge about the grammar rules and context. This has a wide variety of applications and is a field of active research. Also translation between these languages is studied in AI.

4. Vision, Speech recognition and similar areas.

Seeing an animal and recognizing it as a cat is child's play, but a difficult task for computers. Modern AI programs focuses on recognizing objects and persons and behavior based on vision. This has many applications in robot navigation, crime detection, military operations and so on.

5. Expert Systems

Human experts are rare, costly and perishing. If we spend a large sum and train a person as a neurologist, the maximum we can expect is 30-40 years of service. And we cannot take a copy of the neurologist! So if we can train a computer to have the same expertise or to be precise expert behaviour, at least in a narrow field, the utility is high. Expert systems deal with extracting expertise and porting it to computers. That is creating software that can exhibit expert behavior. This field has undergone explosive growth in the last few years.

6.Neural networks

Animal brain is composed of neurons and performs computations (thinking) by passing signals between these networks of neurons. Why not imitate this and evolve intelligence? Neural networks began from this foundation. They are capable of learning, adapting and predicting. Putting in simple language, a neural network is a collection of computation units (real or virtually created), which are interconnected and cooperates for computation. Neural networks have applications in control systems, speech and natural language processing, vision and many other fields.

There are various other areas in AI. It is a vast and emerging field. I will tell more about it in my next article

CHAPTER FIVE

TOOLS AND MACHINE LEARNING LIBARIES REQUIRED TO WORK WITH MACHINE LEARNING

OPERATING SYSTEM

Linux OS was first created by a student from the University of Helsinki in Finland. The creator's name was Linus Torvalds and he had an interest which turned into a passion for Minix, a small Unix application which was later developed into a system that surpassed the Minix standards. He started working on the minix in 1991 and worked heavily until 1994 when the first version of Linux kernal 1.0 was released. This Linux kernal sets the foundation to which the OS of Linux is formed. Hundreds of organizations and companies today have hired individuals and used them to release versions of operating systems using Linux kernal.

Linux's functioning, features and adaptation have made Linux and Windows OS's excellent alternatives to other OS's. IBM and other giant companies around the world support Linux and its ongoing work after a decade from its initial release. The OS is incorporated into microchips using a process called "embedding" and is increasing the performance of appliances and devices.

History of Linux

Through the 1990's some computer savy technicians and hobby insistent people with an interest in computers developed desktop management systems. These systems including GNOME and KDE that run on Linux are available to anyone regardless of the persons motive to use the system. Linus Torvalds was interested in learning the capabilities and features of an 80386 processor for task switching. The application originally named Freax was first used with the Minix operating system.

Both the Freax and Minix designs seemed to be sacrificing performance for academic research and studying. Many of the computing specialists now are making assumptions that have changed since the 90's. Portability is now a common goal for these specialists of the computer industry and this is certainly not a academic requirement for software. Various ports to IA-32,

PowerPC, MIPS, Alpha, and ARM along with supporting products being made and sold to wholesalers and retailers, commercial enterprises gave Linus an Alpha based system when tasks on Linux's priority list moved up to a notably busy point.

History of Windows

Presidents of Microsoft were Bill Gates and Paul Allen, they shared the title until 1977, when Bill Gates became presidnt and Paul Allen vice president. In 1978 the disk drives of the Tandy and Apple machines were 5.25-inch. First COMDEX computer show in Las Vegas introduces a 16-bit microprocessor, and from Intel manufacturers they introduce a 8086 chip. Al Gore comes up with the phrase "information highway." The same year Apple co-founder Steve Wozniak developed the first programming language called Integer Basic, this language was quickly replaced by the Microsoft Applesoft Basic.

Also in 1978, there was a machine that had an integrated, self contained design and was priced at less than $800, known as the Commodore PET which was a Personal Electronic Transactor. On 4/11/78 Microsoft announces its third language product, Microsoft COBOL-80. On the 1st of November in 1978 after their third language introduction, they opened their first international sales office in Japan. Microsoft delegates ASCII Microsoft, located in Tokyo, asits exclusive sales agent for the Far East. And finally on New Years Eve of 1978 Microsoft announced that their year end sales were over $1 million dollars. The following year in April of 1979 Microsoft 8080 BASIC is the first microprocessor to win the ICP Million Dollar Award.

The big computers were dominated by software for the mainframe computer, the recognition for the pc computer indicated growth and acceptance in the industry.

Both Allen and Gates return home to Bellevue, Washington and announce plans to open offices in their home town, thus becoming the first microcomputer software company in the Northwest.

Technical Details of both Linux and Windows OS's

An OS takes care of all input and output coming to a computer. It manages users, processes, memory management, printing, telecommunications, networking, and etc. The OS sends data to a disk, the printer, the screen and other peripherals connected to the computer. A computer can't work without an OS. The OS tells the machine how to process instructions coming from input devices and software running on the computer. Therefore every computer is built different, commands for in or output will have to be treated differently. In most cases an operating system is not a gigantic nest of programs but instead a small system of programs that operate by the core or kernal. The pc computer system is so compact that for these small supporting programs it is easier to rewrite parts r packages of the system than to redesign an entire program.

When first created OS's were designed to help applications interact with the computer hardware. This is the same today, the importance of the OS has risen to the point where the operating system defines the computer. The OS gives off a layer of abstraction between the user and the machine when they communicate. Users don't see the hardware directly, but instead they see it through the OS. This abstraction can be used to hide certain hardware details from the application and the user.

Applied software are not generic but specifically for one single task machine. The software will not run on any other machine. Applications like this are SABRE, the reservation system of airlines, and defense systems. In the case of Computer Aided Software Engineering (CASE), due to the fact that creating software is an expensive and time consuming process, These programs will support and in some cases replace the engineer in creating computer programs. Cad cam systems is the computer aided design &computer aided manufacturing. The electronic drawing board in a computer program whom features are multiplying. Like premanufactured elements, strength calculations, emulations of how a construction will hold in earthquakes.

In Linux there has been a question that has been going back and forth for a while now, is SCSI dead for workstations? There have been many advancements in SATA and the mainstream acceptance of 10K RPM Western Digital Raptor which made SCSI too expensive for what is needed in a workstation. It's time we take a look at Linux. How does the Western Digital Raptor WD740GD compare to the three latest Ultra320 SCSI drives: the Seagate Cheetah 10K.7, Seagate Cheetah 15K.3, and Seagate Cheetah 15K.4. This section covers the technology of the drives, acoustics, heat, size, and performance.

Lets take a look at the latest generation of the Seagate 10K Cheetah line and 15K Cheetah line. We will also be taking an in depth look at the latest 10K SATA drive from Western Digital the 74GB WD740GD. Starting with the Western Digital Raptor, WD pushes this drive as the low cost answer to SCSI. On their website, they like to show off the drives 1,200,000 hours MTBF(Mean Time Between Failure) which matches the last generation MTBF of the Seagate Cheetah 15K.3 and is very close to the reliability rating of today's Cheetahs.

In Linux's datasheet or newsletter, they also mention that the Cheetah drive is designed for "high performance around the clock usage." Both the Cheetah and the Western Digital Raptor drives have the same amount of cache memory. When you are speaking of operations in a multi-tasking/multi-user environment, the benefit of various queuing techniques is an advantage. All Ultra 320 SCSI drives support what is called Native Command Queuing or NCQ. This technique is where all commands sent to the disk drive can be queued up and reordered in the most efficient order. This stops the drive from having to request service on only one side of the disk, then going to the other side of the disk serving another request, in order to return for the next request.. While some of the SATA drives do support NCQ, the Raptor does not. The Raptor does have another form of queuing called Tagged Command Queuing or TCQ. This method is not as effective as NCQ and requires support in both the drive and host controller. From what they have been able to determine, TCQ support is sparse, even under Windows.

The SATA drive has itself backed up on their durability claim by stating their use of fluid dynamic bearings in their drives. The fluid dynamic bearings replace ball bearings to cut down on drive wear and tear and decrease operating noise.

Microsoft Windows XP technologies make it easy to enjoy games, music, and movies in addition to creating movies and enhancing digital photo's. Direct X 9.0 technology drives high speed multimedia and various games on the PC. DirectX provides the exciting graphics, sound, music, and three dimensional animation that bring games to life. Direct X is also the link that allows software engineers to develop a game that is high speed and multimedia driven for your PC. Direct X was introduced in 1995 and it's popularity soared as multimedia application development reached new heights. Today Direct X has progressed to an Application Programming Interface (API) and being applied into Microsoft Windows Operating Systems. This way software developers can access hardware features without having to write hardware code.

Some of the features of the windows media player 9 series with smart jukebox gives users more control over their music. With easy cd transfer to the computer, cd burning and compatibility, available on portable players as well. Users can also discover more with services that have premium entertainment. Windows media player 9 seriers works well with windows xp using the built-in digital media features and delivers a "state of the art" experience.

When Windows Millenium Edition 2000 came out of stores it was specifically designed for home users. It had the first Microsoft version of a video editing product. Movie Maker is used to capture and organize and edit video clips, and then export them for PC or web playback. Movie maker 2, released in 2003, adds new movie making transitions, jazzy titles, and neat special effects. Based on Microsoft Direct Show and Windows Media technologies, Movie Maker was originally included only with Windows Millenium Edition. Now Movie Maker 2 is available for Windows XP Home Edition and Windows XP Professional.

With the release of Windows XP in 2001 came Windows Messenger, bringing instant messaging to users across the internet. Users communicate using Text messages in real time in Windows Messenger. Real time messaging with video conferencing has been available for a long time before now. The first communication tool provided by Windows Messenger used integrated, easy to use text chat, voice, video communication, and data collaboration.

Linux is being developed and thus is freely redistributable in code form. Linux is available and developed over the internet. Many of the engineers who took part in producing it are from over seas and have never meet one another. This operating system is at a source level code and is on a large scale, this crucial features have made possible for this program to become a featureful and stable system.

Eric Raymond has written a popular essay on the development of Linux entitled The Cathedral. and the bazaar. He describes the way the Linux kernal uses a Bazaar approach that has the code released quickly and very often, and that this requires input that has provided improvement to the system. This Bazaar approach is reported to the Cathedral approach used by other systems like GNU Emacs core. The Cathedral approach is characterized by a better code, but unfortunately it is released far less often. A poor opportunity for people outside the group who can not contribute to the process.

Some of the high-lights and success of the Bazaar projects do not include the opening code for everyone to observe, at the design level of the Bazaar. On the same token the Cathedral approach is widely viewed by everyone and is appropriate. Once debugging the code is executed, it is necessary to open the Bazaar to everyone in order to find different errors involving the code. If they can fix the code this a great effort and help to the coders.

Advantages and Disadvantages of the two OS's

The writer of this Linux OS web page Chris Browne, describes the way that Linux efforts are distributed and some of the advantages and disadvantages of the Linux OS. The Linux OS comes with some experimental versions such as the 2.5. x series where version numbers go steadily upwards every week. The stable version changes only when bugs are detected in the system and the bugs must be fixed in the experimental series. This occurrence does not change very often. Linux users know that this happens, and they work to solve the bugs.

It is not guaranteed that all users will immediately fix their problems with the systems if they are not being affected (or don't notice they are affected) by problems, there are fixes quickly available, sometimes distributed across the internet after a few hours of diagnosis. Linux fixes are available more quickly than commercial vendors like Microsoft, HP, and IBM. Usually for Linux this diagnosis is available before they even know there's a problem. This acknowledgement is in contrast to other companies behavior, Bill Gates claims in his press releases that Microsoft code has no bugs. This seems to mean that there are no bugs that Microsoft cares to fix.

Microsoft came to the conclusion that the majority of bugs detected in their systems are present because users don't use their software correctly. The problems that remain for Microsoft are few in number and are caused by actual errors. There is remaining work to get the stable Linux system, with configured Linux kernels that should and do have suitably configured software on top of the workload the systems have to run for hundreds of days without rebooting the computers. Some of the general public as well as computer professionals like engineers and technicians complain that Linux is always changing. Chris says that "effort and interest of the Linux kernal will stop when people want to stop building and enhancing the Linux kernal." As long as new technology and devices like the video cards are being constructed and people interested in Linux will keep coming up with new improvements for Linux, work on Linux OS will progress.

The disadvantage of the Linux OS is that it may end because of the development of better platform for kernal hacking, or because Linux in the future will be so displaced that it becomes unmanageable. This has not happened yet but many researchers state that in the future, with various plans for attaining services to the consumer or business, Linux is moving away from the base kernal and into user space which creates less room for data and information. The announcement of a Debian Hurd effort suggests an alternative to the problem of kernal hacking. The Hurd kernal, which runs and is sent as a set of processes on top of a microkernal such as MACH, may provide a system for those people that are not satisfied with the constant changes of the linux kernal. Mach has a "message passing" abstraction that allows the OS to be created as a set of components that will work in conjunction with one another.

Competetive, Collaborative Efforts

To start this section I'll tell about the beginning of the personal computer and it's roots with IBM. Vertically integrated proprietary de facto standards architectures were the norm for the first three decades of the postwar computer industry. Each computer manufacturer made most if not all of its technology internally, and sold that technology as part of an integrated computer. This systems era was ascendant from IBM's 1964 introduction of its System 360 until the release of the 1981, personal computer from IBM. This was challenged by two different approaches. One was the fragmentation of proprietary standards in the PC industry between different suppliers, which led Microsoft and Intel to seek industry wide dominance for their proprietary component of the overall system architecture, making what Moschella (1997) terms the "PC era" (1964-1981). The second was a movement by users and second tier producers to construct industrywide "open" systems, in which the standard was not owned by a single firm.

The adoption of the Linux system in the late 1990s was a response to these earlier approaches. Linux was the most commercially accepted example of a new wave of "open source" software, the software and the source code are freely distributed to use and modify. The advantages of Linux in contrast to the proprietary PC standards, particularly software standards controlled by Microsoft. Product compatibility standards have typically been considered using a simple unidemensional typology, bifurcated between "compatible" and "incompatible." Further more, to illuminate differences between proprietary and open standards strategies, Gabel's (1987) multi-dimensional classification attribute, with each dimension assuming one of several (discrete) levels:

"multivintage" compatibility between successive generations of a product:

"product line" compatibility, providing interoperability across the breadth of the company's

product line-as Microsoft has with its Windows CE, 95/98/ME, and NT/2000 product families.

"multivendors" compatibility, i.e. compatibility of products between competing producers.

The first successful multi-vendor operating system was Unix, developed by a computer science research group at Bell Telephone Laboratories (BTL) in New Jersey beginning in 1969. As with the earlier Multics research project between MIT, BTL and mainframe computer maker General Electric, Unix was a multi-user time-shared OS designed as a research project by programmers for their personal use. Other characteristics key to

116

Unix's success reflected path dependencies by its developers and early users

AT&T was forbidden by its 1956 consent decree from being in the computer business, so it did not sell the OS commercially. After publishing research papers, Bell Labs was flooded with requests from university computer science departments, who received user licenses and source code but a lack of support. Along cam budget constraints that limited BTL researchers to DEC minicomputers opposed to large mainframe computers, Unix was simpler and more efficient than its Multics predecessor, based on the simplified C programming language rather than the more widely used PL/I. Although originally developed DEC minicomputers, Unix was converted to run on other models by users who found programmer time less expensive than buying a supported model, thus setting the stage for it to become a hardware-independent OS.

As they evolved their versions of Unix, fragmentation of Unix developers and adopters into rival "BSD" and "AT&T" camps.

AT&T Unix provided a multivendor standard which, when coupled with the BSD advancements, helped spur the adoption of networked computing. Helped by Sun, whose slogan is "the network is the computer," Unix rapidly gained acceptance during the 1980s as the preferred OS for networked engineering workstations , At the same time, it became a true multivendor standard as minicomputer producers with a small amount of customers, weak R&D and immature OS licensed Unix from AT&T. The main exceptions to the Unix push were the early leaders in workstations (Apollo) and minicomputers (DEC), who used their proprietary OS as a source of competitive advantage, and were the last to switch to Unix in their respective segments.

Some of the advocates from the two producers formed a number of trade associations to promote Unix and related operating systems. In doing so they fueled the adoption and standardization of Unix, hoping to increase the amount of application software to compete with sponsored, proprietary architectures.

These two groups promoted these under the rubric "open systems"; the editors of a book series on such systems summarized their goals as follows:

Open systems allow users to move their applications between systems easily; purchasing decisions can be made on the basis of cost-performance ratio and vendor support, rather than on systems which run a users application suite .

Despite these goals, the Unix community spent the 1980s and early 1990s fragmented into AT&T and Berkeley warring factions, each of which sought control of the OS API's to maximize the software available for their versions. Each faction had its own adherents. To avoid paying old earlier mainframe switching costs, U.S. Department of Defense procurement decisions began to favor Unix over proprietary systems. As AT&T formalized its System V Interface Definition and encouraged hardware makers to adopt System V, it became the multivendor standard required by DoD procurements

BSD group was only developed for DEC minicomputers, its Unix variant was not multivendor and less attractive and appealing for DoD procurements. The numerous innovations of the BSD group in terms of usability, software development tools and networking made it more attractive to university computer scientists for their own research and teaching, making it the OS minicomputer preferred by computer science departments in the U.S., Europe and Japan (Salus 1994). The divergent innovation meant that the two major Unix variants differed in terms of internal structure, user commands and application programming interfaces (APIs). It was the latter difference that most seriously affected computer buyers, as custom software developed for one type of Unix could not directly be recompiled on the other, adding switching costs between the two systems. Also, both the modem-based and DARPA networking facilitated the distribution of user donated source code libraries, that were free but often required site-specific custom programming if the Unix API's at the users site differed from those of faced by the original contributor.

Microsoft Windows continues to invest in products based on the Itanium processor family, and the Itanium Solutions Alliance will further this investment by helping the growth of the ecosystem of applications and solutions available on Windows platform and SQL Server 2005," quoting Bob Kelly, general manager, Windows infrastructure, Microsoft Corp. "We look forward to working with the members of the Itanium Solutions Alliance to help IT managers transition from RISC-based Unix servers to Itanium based systems running on the Windows platform.

How to Become a .NET Developer

So you want to know how to become a .NET developer either because there is a position you want that requires you to have these skills or perhaps you're just interested in .NET development. It is after all one of the mostly widely used languages for development. This article will serve as an How To guide for anyone who wants to become a .NET developer through the use of resources such as: books, development tools, and links. These are the absolute must haves for aspiring .NET developers:

Learning .NET Develpment

The latest version of the .NET framework is 3.5. The Beginner's Guide to Beginning ASP.NET 3.5: In C# and VB is part of a series of books written by programmers for programmers. It's a comprehensible book on development using .NET 3.5. is written for people who have never done any programming. It takes you step by step, teaching you first the basics, then the more complex tasks, and also some best practices. Even though 3.5 is the latest version, .NET 2.0 is still widely used. The examples are in both C# and VB. By reading this book you could literally build a web site from scratch in which ever one you choose.

ASP.NET 3.5 In C# and VB

.NET Development Tools

The Integrated Devclopent Fnvironment or IDE used for .NET Development is Microsoft Visual Studio. The latest version is Visual Studio 2008. There are many editions of this tool but I'll just focus on two: the free one and the not so free one. For those of you with a few hundred or maybe thousand to spend or an organization willing to spend that much there is Visual Studio 2008:

Visual Studio 2008

While you could down grade and get the now cheaper 2005 version of Visual Studio, in order to maximize .NET 3.5's programming features you will have to the 2008 version. It can range any where from a $200+ for the Standard Edition to $4,000+ for the Team System Edition. OR if you're not so inclined to spend your money, you have two options: download thc trial version or Visual Studio Express which is FREE:

Visual Studio 2008 Express

The Express version is definitely good enough to create and launch a web application, but it does have its limitations, so beware. See the at the end of this article for some free tools that make up for some of these limitiation.

Database Tools

While .NET applications can use many different types of database such as Oracle, Access, or MySQL, the most commonly used is Microsoft SQL Server. The latest version is SQL Server 2008.

SQL Server 2008

Once again you have the choice of buying one of the official version of SQL Server, these range anywhere from $40+ to $1600+ depending on which version you get; or downloading the free version SQL Server Management Studio Express.

SQL Server Management Studio Express

There are limitations in the free version, of course, but using the Express version poses little trouble only on your development machine or small applications. Once you get into bigger applications or running jobs and other complicated process, a pricier version of SQL Server might be required.

BONUS: Top 5 FREE Tools for .NET Development

If you're a complete novice to programming you might want to bookmark this page and comeback to this list later. These tools will come in handy once you actually get into development.

As you might or might not already know, .NET development can get rather expensive; compared to the other languages like Java, which has a free IDE: Eclipse. In any case, here are some most free open source tools that will make your life A LOT easier.

1. NUnit

Unit Testing is a must for any serious developer who wants to put out functional, bug free applications. Microsoft offers its tool for unit testing, MSTest, but only in certain versions of Visual Studio. NUnit is the .NET version of Java's JUnit, an open source unit testing framework.

2. NAnt

Deploying a website can be a hassle. There are connection strings to update, configuration files to change. NAnt makes these things easier by automating these various changes. Like NUnit, its the .NET version of Java Ant.

3. CruiseControl.NET

As your application grows and you continue adding new features, it is always important to integrate your new code with your old code and ensure that everything works. CruiseControl.NET helps with this through its Automated Continuous Integration Server. CruiseControl.NET, the .NET version of CruiseControl for Java, works in conjunction with NAnt to anything from running your unit tests each time you add new code to emailing you if someone checks in bad code that breaks the build.

4. NHibernate

This isn't necessarily a tool, so much as it's a framework. Once again this is a .NET port of the Java based Hibernate. NHiberante acts as the persistence layer between your application and its database. In order not to write long complicated SQL statements, NHibernate is perfect. It allows to write the usually tedious select statements or the very complex join statements in a fraction of the team. Micrsoft's LINQ can also be used in the same way.

5. Mono

Last but definitely not least is Mono. Do you for whatever reason not have IIS or do you want to use other platforms like Linux or OS X? Well you're in luck, Mono, which is sponsored by Novell, offers an alternative to IIS for those not using Windows.

.NET is an awesome framework. It is very powerful and there are tons of libraries that allows you to do some amazing things. Once you learn it, you'll be able to do a lot. One thing to note though: some lists of system requirements might tell you that you only need to have 1 GB of memory to run all of the tools such as SQL Server and Visual Studio. My suggestion is that you at least get 2 GB of memory on your development machine. As cool as they are, the applications can be resource hogs and you want to make sure you're developing efficiently

CHAPTER SIX

DECISION TREES IN RELATION TO MACHINE LEARNING

PYTHON

Python is a general-purpose high-level programming language which is also defined as multi-paradigm programming language for its support for object-oriented programming, structured programming, functional programming as well as aspect-oriented programming among others.

It was first implemented in 1989 by Guido Van Rossum in 1989 but gained huge popularity in the 2000s. In contrast to Perl and Ruby's philosophy of "many ways of doing a thing", Python's motto " "There should be one -- and preferably only one -- obvious way to do it." is a direct challenge to Perl as well as Ruby and factored majorly in the competition between the two new generation languages. However, what sets Python apart is the strict layout of the language. But Python code is easy to read, almost making it look like pseudo-code, so it is easy to learn for beginners and offers the best readability to experienced programmers. Python also has a wide collection of libraries, the official repository of Python libraries (Python Package Index) offers functionalities as diverse as graphical user interfaces, multimedia, web frameworks, databases connectivity, networking and communication, system administration, test frameworks, automation, text and image processing, scientific computing to name a few. Also Python is compatible with most number of platforms and is bundled with most Linux distributions.

POPULARITY OF PYTHON OVER RUBY

While both Python and Ruby had been around for some time, Ruby gained popularity with the arrival of the Ruby on Rails framework in 2005. By the time, Python had already established itself as a programmer-friendly and powerful language and created a niche for itself. Although, even now Ruby on Rails remains a more popular framework over Python's Django, it also means Ruby has remained restricted to web development framework while Python has diversified and emerged as the preferred language in several other areas. Python has also gathered a larger community of users loyal to it and a large repository of library modules and documentation. While Ruby too has some very dedicated programmers championing for it, the fact remains that Python still manages to have a larger community of collaborators.

One of the key reasons of Python's popularity is its language architecture which makes it easier to both write and read code. Since it is easy to learn, a lot of beginners are adopting it and schools and colleges are including it as part of their syllabus. As readability of code is a strong merit of Python, experienced programmers are adopting it too to cut down time in maintaining and upgrading code. Furthermore, Python runs well in most platforms and is included as a standard component with most Linux distributions, FreeBSD, NetBSD, OpenBSD, OS X and AmigaOS4 and is fully compatible with other OSes including Windows which makes the accessibility of the language to the programmers easy and encourages beginners to explore it. From a simple web research it seems clear that Python is emerging as the more popular language from among the two new generation programming languages.

According to Wikipedia, Python has remained in the top eight most popular languages since 2008 in TIOBE Programming Community Index indicating that its popularity has been very consistent. In TIOBE Index for July 2015, Python occupies the 5th position while Ruby has been pushed down to the 15th. It would thus be safe to conclude that Python is much more popular than Ruby.

LEARNING FROM DATA - LOGISTIC REGRESSION WITH L2 REGULARIZATION IN PYTHON

Logistic Regression

Logistic regression is used for binary classification problems -- where you have some examples that are "on" and other examples that are "off." You get as input a training set; which has some examples of each class along with a label saying whether each example is "on" or "off". The goal is to learn a model from the training data so that you can predict the label of new examples that you haven't seen before and don't know the label of.

For one example, suppose that you have data describing a bunch of buildings and earthquakes (E.g., year the building was constructed, type of material used, strength of earthquake,etc), and you know whether each building collapsed ("on") or not ("off") in each past earthquake. Using this data, you'd like to make predictions about whether a given building is going to collapse in a hypothetical future earthquake.

One of the first models that would be worth trying is logistic regression.

Coding it up

I wasn't working on this exact problem, but I was working on something close. Being one to practice what I preach, I started looking for a dead simple Python logistic regression class. The only requirement is that I wanted it to support L2 regularization (more on this later). I'm also sharing this code with a bunch of other people on many platforms, so I wanted as few dependencies on external libraries as possible.

I couldn't find exactly what I wanted, so I decided to take a stroll down memory lane and implement it myself. I've written it in C++ and Matlab before but never in Python.

I won't do the derivation, but there are plenty of good explanations out there to follow if you're not afraid of a little calculus. Just do a little Googling for "logistic regression derivation." The big idea is to write down the probability of the data given some setting of internal parameters, then to take the derivative, which will tell you how to change the internal parameters to make the data more likely.

For those of you out there that know logistic regression inside and out, take a look at how short the train method is.

Regularization

Regularization is a good idea.

Let me drive home the point. Take a look at the results of running the code (linked at the bottom).

Take a look at the top row.

On the left side, you have the training set. There are 25 examples laid out along the x axis, and the y axis tells you if the example is "on" (1) or "off" (0). For each of these examples, there's a vector describing its attributes that I'm not showing. After training the model, I ask the model to ignore the known training set labels and to estimate the probability that each label is "on" based only on the examples's description vectors and what the model has learned (hopefully things like stronger earthquakes and older buildings increase the likelihood of collapse).

The probabilities are shown by the red X's. In the top left, the red X's are right on top of the blue dots, so it is very sure about the labels of the examples, and it's always correct.

Now on the right side, we have some new examples that the model hasn't seen before. This is called the test set. This is essentially the same as the left side, but the model knows nothing about the test set class labels (yellow dots). What you see is that it still does a decent job of predicting the labels, but there are some troubling cases where it is very confident and very wrong. This is known as overfitting.

This is where regularization comes in. As you go down the rows, there is stronger L2 regularization -- or equivalently, pressure on the internal parameters to be zero. This has the effect of reducing the model's certainty. Just because it can perfectly reconstruct the training set doesn't mean that it has everything figured out. You can imagine that if you were relying on this model to make important decisions, it would be desirable to have at least a bit of regularization in there.

And here's the code. It looks long, but most of it is to generate the data and plot the results. The bulk of the work is done in the train method, which is only three (dense) lines. It requires numpy, scipy, and pylab.

For full disclosure, I should admit that I generated my random data in a way such that it is susceptible to overfitting, possibly making logistic-regression-without-regularization look worse than it is.

THE PYTHON CODE

```python
from scipy.optimize.optimize import fmin_cg, fmin_bfgs, fmin

import numpy as np

def sigmoid(x):

    return 1.0 / (1.0 + np.exp(-x))

class SyntheticClassifierData():
    def __init__(self, N, d):

        """ Create N instances of d dimensional input vectors and a 1D
```

```python
        class label (-1 or 1). """



        means = .05 * np.random.randn(2, d)



        self.X_train = np.zeros((N, d))


        self.Y_train = np.zeros(N)


        for i in range(N):


            if np.random.random() > .5:


                y = 1
```

```python
        else:

            y = 0


        self.X_train[i, :] = np.random.random(d) + means[y,
:]


        self.Y_train[i] = 2.0 * y - 1


    self.X_test = np.zeros((N, d))


    self.Y_test = np.zeros(N)


    for i in range(N):


        if np.random.randn() > .5:
```

```python
            y = 1

        else:

            y = 0

        self.X_test[i, :] = np.random.random(d) + means[y, :]

        self.Y_test[i] = 2.0 * y - 1


class LogisticRegression():
```

A simple logistic regression model with L2 regularization (zero-mean Gaussian priors on parameters).

```python
    def __init__(self, x_train=None, y_train=None,
x_test=None, y_test=None,



        alpha=.1, synthetic=False):




        # Set L2 regularization strength



        self.alpha = alpha




        # Set the data.



        self.set_data(x_train, y_train, x_test, y_test)




        # Initialize parameters to zero, for lack of a better
choice.
```

```python
        self.betas = np.zeros(self.x_train.shape[1])


    def negative_lik(self, betas):


        return -1 * self.lik(betas)


    def lik(self, betas):



        """ Likelihood of the data under the current settings of
parameters. """


        # Data likelihood


        l = 0
```

```python
    for i in range(self.n):

        l += log(sigmoid(self.y_train[i] *

                         np.dot(betas, self.x_train[i,:])))

    # Prior likelihood

    for k in range(1, self.x_train.shape[1]):

        l -= (self.alpha / 2.0) * self.betas[k]**2

    return l

def train(self):
```

""" Define the gradient and hand it off to a scipy gradient-based

optimizer. """

Define the derivative of the likelihood with respect to beta_k.

Need to multiply by -1 because we will be minimizing.

```
dB_k = lambda B, k : np.sum([-self.alpha * B[k] +

                self.y_train[i] * self.x_train[i, k] *

                sigmoid(-self.y_train[i] *
```

```python
                    np.dot(B, self.x_train[i,:]))



                for i in range(self.n)]) * -1




        # The full gradient is just an array of componentwise
derivatives


        dB = lambda B : np.array([dB_k(B, k)



                        for k in range(self.x_train.shape[1])])




        # Optimize



        self.betas = fmin_bfgs(self.negative_lik, self.betas,
fprime=dB)
```

```python
def set_data(self, x_train, y_train, x_test, y_test):

    """ Take data that's already been generated. """

    self.x_train = x_train

    self.y_train = y_train

    self.x_test = x_test

    self.y_test = y_test

    self.n = y_train.shape[0]
```

```python
def training_reconstruction(self):

    p_y1 = np.zeros(self.n)

    for i in range(self.n):

        p_y1[i] = sigmoid(np.dot(self.betas, self.x_train[i,:]))

    return p_y1

def test_predictions(self):

    p_y1 = np.zeros(self.n)

    for i in range(self.n):
```

```python
            p_y1[i] = sigmoid(np.dot(self.betas, self.x_test[i,:]))


        return p_y1



    def plot_training_reconstruction(self):


        plot(np.arange(self.n), .5 + .5 * self.y_train, 'bo')


        plot(np.arange(self.n), self.training_reconstruction(),
'rx')


        ylim([-.1, 1.1])


    def plot_test_predictions(self):


        plot(np.arange(self.n), .5 + .5 * self.y_test, 'yo')
```

```python
        plot(np.arange(self.n), self.test_predictions(), 'rx')


        ylim([-.1, 1.1])


if __name__ == "__main__":


    from pylab import *


    # Create 20 dimensional data set with 25 points -- this will
be


    # susceptible to overfitting.


    data = SyntheticClassifierData(25, 20)


    # Run for a variety of regularization strengths
```

```python
alphas = [0, .001, .01, .1]


for j, a in enumerate(alphas):




        # Create a new learner, but use the same data for each
run


        lr = LogisticRegression(x_train=data.X_train,
y_train=data.Y_train,


                        x_test=data.X_test, y_test=data.Y_test,


                        alpha=a)
```

```
print "Initial likelihood:"

print lr.lik(lr.betas

# Train the model

lr.train()

# Display execution info

print "Final betas:"

print lr.betas

print "Final lik:"
```

```
print lr.lik(lr.betas)
```

```
# Plot the results
```

```
subplot(len(alphas), 2, 2*j + 1)
```

```
lr.plot_training_reconstruction()
```

```
ylabel("Alpha=%s" % a)
```

```
if j == 0:
```

```
    title("Training set reconstructions")
```

```
subplot(len(alphas), 2, 2*j + 2)


lr.plot_test_predictions()


if j == 0:


    title("Test set predictions")


show(
```

CHAPTER SEVEN

WHY IS PYTHON HERE TO STAY?

Python was originally conceived by Van Rossum as a hobby language in December 1989. Also, the major and backward-incompatible version of the general-purpose programming language was released on 3rd December 2008. But Python is recently rated by a number of surveyors as the most popular coding language of 2015. The massive popularity indicates Python's effectiveness as a modern programming language. At the same time, Python 3 is currently used by developers across the worlds for creating a variety of desktop GUI, web and mobile applications. There are also numbers of reasons why the huge popularity and market share of Python will remain intact over a longer period of time.

8 Reasons Why the Massive Popularity of Python Will Remain Intact in the Future

1) Supports Multiple Programming Paradigms,

Skilled developers often take advantage of different programming paradigms to reduce the amount of time and efforts required for developing large and complex applications. Like others modern programming languages, Python also supports a number of commonly used programming styles including object-oriented, functional, procedural and imperative. It further features automatic memory management, along with a dynamic type system. So programmers can use the language to effectuate development of large and complex software applications.

2) Doesn't Require Programmers to Write Lengthy Code,

Python is designed with complete focus on code readability. So the programmer can create a readable base code that can be used by members of distributed teams. At the same time, the simple syntax of the programming language enables them to express concepts without writing long lines of code. This feature makes it easier for developers to create large and complex applications within a stipulated amount of time. As they can easily skip certain tasks required by other programming languages, it becomes easier for developers to maintain and updates their applications.

3) Provides a Comprehensive Standard Library,

Python further scores over other programming languages due to its extensive standard library. Programmers can use these libraries to accomplish a variety of tasks without writing long lines of code. Also, the standard library of Python is designed with a large number of frequently used programming tasks scripted into it. Thus, it helps programmers to accomplish tasks like string operations, development and implementation of web services, working with internet protocols, and handling operating system interface.

4) Effectuates Web Application Development,

Python is designed as a general-purpose programming language, and lacks built-in web development features. But web developers use a variety of add-on modules to write modern web applications in Python. While writing in Python, programmers have option to use several high-level web frameworks including Django, web2py, TurboGears, CubicWeb, and Reahl. These web frameworks help programmers to perform a number of operations, without writing additional code, like database manipulation, URL routing, session storage, retrieval, and output template formatting. They can further use the web framework to protect web applications from cross-site scripting attacks, SQL injection, and cross-site request forgery.

5) Facilitates Development of High Quality GUI, Scientific and Numeric Applications,

Python is currently available with the major operating systems like Windows, Mac OS X, Linux and UNIX. So the desktop GUI applications written in the programming language can be deployed on multiple platforms. The programmer can speedup cross-platform desktop GUI application development using frameworks like Kivy, wxPython and PyGtk. A number of reports have highlighted that Python is used widely for development of numeric and scientific applications. Writing in Python, the developers can take advantage of tools like Scipy, Pandas, IPython, along with the Python Imaging Library.

6) Simplifies Prototyping of Applications,

Nowadays, organizations want to beat the competition by developing software with distinct and innovative features. That is why; prototyping has become an integral part of modern software development lifecycle. Before writing the code, developers have to create prototype of the application to display its features and functionality to various stakeholders. As a simple and fast programming language, Python enables programmers to develop the final system without putting any extra time and effort. At the same time, the developer have the option to start developing the system directly from the prototype simply by refactoring the code.

7) Can also be used for Mobile App Development,

Frameworks like Kivy also make Python usable for developing mobile apps. As a library, Kivy can be used for creating both desktop applications and mobile apps. But it allows developers to write the code once, and deploy the same code on multiple platforms. Along with interfacing with the hardware of the mobile device, Kivy also comes with a built-in camera adapter, modules to render and play videos, and modules to accept user input through multi-touch and gestures. Thus, programmers can use Kivy to create multiples versions of the same application for iOS, Android and Windows Phone. Also, the framework does not require developers to write long lines of code while creating Kivy programs.

8) Open Source

Despite being rated as the most popular coding language of 2015, Python is still available as open source and free software. Along with large IT companies, startups and freelance software developers can also use the programming language without paying any fees or royalty. Python makes everything easier for businesses to reduce development cost significantly. At the same time, the programmer can also have the assistance of a large and active community to add(in adding) out-of-box features to the software application.

The last major release of Python took place in December 2008. Python 3 was released as a backward-incompatible version with most of the major features back ported to Python 2.6 and 2.7. However, the programming language is being updated by the community at regular intervals. The community released

Python 3.4.3 on 23rd February with several features and patches. So the developer can always use the most recent version of the Python programming language to effectuate development of various software applications

CHAPTER EIGHT

IMPORTANT PYTHON FRAMEWORKS FOR DEVELOPERS

As a dynamic, general purpose and object-oriented programming language, Python is used widely by developers across the world to build a variety of software applications. Unlike other modern programming languages, Python enables programmers to express concept with readable code. The users also have an option to integrate Python with other popular programming languages and tools seamlessly. But it cannot be used directly to write different types of software.

Python developers Often have to use a variety of frameworks and tools to build high quality software applications within a shorter amount of time. The resources provided by the Python frameworks help users to reduce the time and effort required for modern applications. They also have an option to choose from a number of frameworks according to the nature and requirements of individual projects. However, it is also important for the programmers to know some of the Python frameworks that will remain popular in the longer run.

10 Python Frameworks that will Remain Popular

1) Kivy

As an open source Python library, Kivy makes it easier for programmers to build multi-touch user interfaces. It supports a number of popular platforms including Windows, Linux, OS X, iOS and Android. So the cross-platform framework enables users to create the app for multiple platforms using the same code base. It is also designed with features to take advantage of the native inputs, protocols and devices. Kivy further includes a fast graphic engine, while allowing users to choose from more than 20 extensible widgets.

2) Qt

The open source Python framework is written in C++. Qt allows developers to build connected applications and UIs that run on multiple operating systems and devices. Developers can further create cross-platform applications and UIs without making any changes to the code. Qt further scores over other frameworks due to its comprehensive library of APIs and tools. Programmers have option to use Qt either under the community license or the commercial license.

3) PyGU

PyGUI is considered to be simpler than other Python frameworks. But it enables developers to create GUI API by taking advantage of the language features of Python. PyGUI currently supports Windows, OS X and Linux. So developers can use it to create lightweight GUI APIs that can be implemented on these three platforms. They can further document the API comprehensively without referring to the documentation of any third-party GUI library.

4) WxPython

The GUI toolkit for Python helps programmers to create applications with highly functional graphical user interfaces. As wxPython supports Windows, Linux and OS X, it becomes easier for developers to run the same program in multiple platforms without modifying the code. Users can write programs in Python, while taking advantage of the 2D path drawing engine, standard dialogs, dockable windows and other features provided by the framework.

5) Django

Django is the most popular high-level web application development framework for Python. Despite being open source, Django provides a simple and rapid development environment for building a variety of websites and web applications rapidly. It further helps programmers to create web application without writing lengthy code. It further comes with features to prevent some of the common security mistakes made by developers.

6) CherryPy

As a minimalist web framework, CherryPy enables programs to create websites and web applications just like writing other object-oriented Python programs. So it becomes easier for developers to build web applications without writing lengthy code. CherryPy further comes with a clean interface, while allowing developers to decide the right frontend utilities and data storage option. Despite being the oldest Python web application development framework in the market, CherryPy is still being used by programmers to create a variety of modern websites.

7) Flask

Flask is one of the micro web frameworks available for Python. Its core is simple and easy to use, but highly extensible. It also lacks many features provided by other web frameworks including database abstraction layer and form validations. Also, it does not allow users to add common functionality to the web application through third-party libraries. However, Flask enables programmers to create website rapidly by using extensions and code snippets. The snippets and patterns contributed by other members help developers to accomplish common tasks like database access, caching, file upload and authentication without writing any additional code.

8) Pyramid

Despite being a lightweight and simple Python web framework, Pyramid is hugely popular among programmers due to its high and rapid performance. The open source framework can be used to create a variety of applications. Once the standard Python development environment is set up, the developers can use Pyramid to build the applications rapidly. Pyramid further allows users to take advantage of an independent Model-view-controller (MVC) structure. At the same time, they can further take advantage of other frameworks by integrating them with Pyramid.

9) Web.py

As a simple but powerful web framework for Python, web.py helps programmers to build a variety of modern web applications rapidly. The combination of simple architecture and impressive development potential further helps users to overcome some of the common restrictions and inconveniences in web development. It still lacks many features provided by other modern web frameworks. But developers can easily integrate web.py with other frameworks to avail a number of advanced features and functionality.

10) TurboGears

As a highly-scalable web application development framework for Python, TurboGears helps users to eliminate restrictions and limitations within the development environment. It can be used as a micro-framework or full-stack framework. It further provides a flexible object relationship mapper (ORM), along with supporting several databases, multiple data exchange formats, and horizontal data partitioning. Developers can further use the new widget system provided by TurboGears to effectuate development of AJAX-heavy web applications.

On the whole, Python developers have option to choose from many frameworks. Some of these frameworks effectuate development of GUI desktop applications, whereas others help programmers to build modern websites and web application rapidly. At the same time, developers also have option to use certain frameworks to write mobile apps in Python. That is why; it becomes essential for developer to assess the suitability of each framework for his project based on its features and functionality. The user can also consider integrating the framework with other frameworks and tools to avail more advanced features and functionality.

CHAPTER NINE

WHAT IS NEW IN PYTHON PROGRAMMING?

In the today's workplace, Python training is an important part of a programmer's education. As a dynamic language whose design philosophy revolves around readability and conciseness, Python is a popular choice as a scripting language. Like other interpretative languages, it is more flexible than compiled languages, and it can be used to tie disparate systems together. Indeed, Python is a versatile language with many applications in growing fields.

For example, Python is a popular programming language for educational software. Raspberry Pi, the single-board computer project for teaching students computer programming, uses Python as its primary programming language. In addition, much of the software for the One Laptop per Child XO is written in Python. Python is also a very effective language for scientific computing and mathematical software for theoretical mathematics. As educational software development continues to grow, Python will become a more and more important language to know.

In addition to educational software, Python is also the favorite language for any kind of task. Python is a scripting language with processing tools, module architecture, and syntax simplicity, it is a natural choice for applications involving natural language processing. Programs like Wolfram Alpha and Siri are just starting to penetrate the end-user market and many programs yet to come will be written in Python.

Moreover, Python is often used as a scripting language for web applications. For example, Google has adopted Python as one of the available languages in its Google App Engine, a cloud computing platform for developing and hosting web applications. Python is also used as a framework to program communications between computers for web applications like Dropbox.

Python is also quite useful as a modern scripting language similar to Perl, which can be used to tie disparate systems together. Because of this, Python is a standard component for many Linux and Unix based operating systems, It's used extensively in the information security industry, Python is an important tool for systems administrators to learn, as well as programmers.

Python training is becoming an increasingly vital programming language. Due to its versatility, Python has a wide variety of uses in many growing fields. Both programmers and systems administrators would do well to pick up some Python savvy in order to keep their skills up-to-date.

THE EVOLUTION OF PYTHON LANGUAGE OVER THE YEARS

Python is also object-oriented and open source. At the same time, a good number of developers across the world have been making use of Python to create GUI applications, websites and mobile apps. The differentiating factor that Python brings to the table is that it enables programmers to flesh out concepts by writing less and readable code. The developers can further take advantage of several Python frameworks to mitigate the time and effort required for building large and complex software applications.

The programming language is currently being used by a number of high-traffic websites including Google, Yahoo

Groups, Yahoo Maps, Linux Weekly News, Shopzilla and Web Therapy. Likewise, Python also finds great use for creating gaming, financial, scientific and educational applications. However, developers still use different versions of the programming language. According to the usage statistics and market share data of Python posted on W3techs, currently Python 2 is being used by 99.4% of websites, whereas Python 3 is being used only by 0.6% of websites. That is why, it becomes essential for each programmer to understand different versions of Python, and its evolution over many years.

How Python Has Been Evolving over the Years?

Conceived as a Hobby Programming Project

Despite being one of the most popular coding languages of 2015, Python was originally conceived by Guido van Rossum as a hobby project in December 1989. As Van Rossum's office remained closed during Christmas, he was looking for a hobby project that will keep him occupied during the holidays. He planned to create an interpreter for a new scripting language, and named the project as Python. Thus, Python was originally designed as a successor to ABC programming language. After writing the interpreter, Van Rossum made the code public in February 1991. However, at present the open source programming language is being managed by the Python Software Foundation.

Version 1 of Python

Python 1.0 was released in January 1994. The major release included a number of new features and functional programming tools including lambda, filter, map and reduce. The version 1.4 was released with several new features like keyword arguments, built-in support for complex numbers, and a basic form of data hiding. The major release was followed by two minor releases, version 1.5 in December 1997 and version 1.6 in September 2000. The version 1 of Python lacked the features offered by popular programming languages of the time. But the initial versions created a solid foundation for development of a powerful and futuristic programming language.

Version 2 of Python

In October 2000, Python 2.0 was released with the new list comprehension feature and a garbage collection system. The syntax for the list comprehension feature was inspired by other functional programming languages like Haskell. But Python 2.0, unlike Haskell, gave preference to alphabetic keywords over punctuation characters. Also, the garbage collection system effectuated collection of reference cycles. The major release was followed by several minor releases. These releases added a number of functionality to the programming language like support for nested scopes, and unification of Python's classes and types into a single hierarchy. The Python Software Foundation has already announced that there would be no

Python 2.8. However, the Foundation will provide support to version 2.7 of the programming language till 2020.

Version 3 of Python

Python 3.0 was released in December 2008. It came with a several new features and enhancements, along with a number of deprecated features. The deprecated features and backward incompatibility make version 3 of Python completely different from earlier versions. So many developers still use Python 2.6 or 2.7 to avail the features deprecated from last major release. However, the new features of Python 3 made it more modern and popular. Many developers even switched to version 3.0 of the programming language to avail these awesome features.

Python 3.0 replaced print statement with the built-in print() function, while allowing programmers to use custom separator between lines. Likewise, it simplified the rules of ordering comparison. If the operands are not organized in a natural and meaningful order, the ordering comparison operators can now raise a TypeError exception. The version 3 of the programming language further uses text and data instead of Unicode and 8-bit strings. While treating all code as Unicode by default it represents binary data as encoded Unicode.

As Python 3 is backward incompatible, the programmers cannot access features like string exceptions, old-style classes, and implicit relative imports. Also, the developers must be familiar with changes made to syntax and APIs. They can use a tool called "2to3" to migrate their application from Python 2 to 3 smoothly. The tool highlights incompatibility and areas of concern through comments and warnings. The comments help programmers to make changes to the code, and upgrade their existing applications to the latest version of programming language.

Latest Versions of Python

Nowadays, programmers can choose either version 3.4.3 or 2.7.10 of Python. Python 2.7 enables developers to avail improved numeric handling and enhancements for standard library. The version further makes it easier for developers to migrate to Python 3. On the other hand, Python 3.4 comes with several new features and library modules, security improvements and CPython implementation improvements. However, a number of features are deprecated in both Python API and programming language. The developers can still use Python 3.4 to avail support in the longer run.

Version 4 of Python

Python 4.0 is expected to be available in 2023 after the release of Python 3.9. It will come with features that will help programmers to switch from version 3 to 4 seamlessly. Also, as they gain experience, the expert Python developers can take advantage of a number of backward compatible features to modernize their existing applications without putting any extra time and effort. However, developers still have to wait many years to get a clear picture of Python 4.0. However, they must monitor the latest releases to easily migrate to the version 4.0 of the popular coding language.

The version 2 and version 3 of Python are completely different from each other. So each programmer must understand the features of these distinct versions, and compare their functionality based on specific needs of the project. Also, he needs to check the version of Python that each framework supports. However, each developer must take advantage of the latest version of Python to avail new features and long-term support.

www.ingramcontent.com/pod-product-compliance
Lightning Source LLC
Chambersburg PA
CBHW071129050326
40690CB00008B/1395